Andrew Cate is a personal trainer and online weight-loss coach. He writes for several magazines and websites, and can be heard regularly on radio sharing his passion for health, food and fitness. Many people have found success with his books *Throw Out Your Scales*, *Walk Off Weight*, *Lighten Up* and *The H-Factor Diet*.

THE
TIGHT
AR$E
DIET

ANDREW CATE

ABC
Books

The ABC 'Wave' device is a trademark of the Australian Broadcasting Corporation and is used under licence by HarperCollins*Publishers* Australia.

First published in Australia in 2010
by HarperCollins*Publishers* Australia Pty Limited
ABN 36 009 913 517
harpercollins.com.au

HarperCollins*Publishers*
25 Ryde Road, Pymble, Sydney, NSW 2073, Australia
31 View Road, Glenfield, Auckland 0627, New Zealand
A 53, Sector 57, Noida, UP, India
77–85 Fulham Palace Road, London W6 8JB, United Kingdom
2 Bloor Street East, 20th floor, Toronto, Ontario M4W 1A8, Canada
10 East 53rd Street, New York NY 10022, USA

National Library of Australia Cataloguing-in-Publication data:

Cate, Andrew.
    The tight arse diet : lose weight, save money, live well / Andrew Cate.
    ISBN: 9780733327773 (pbk)
    Weight loss—Economic aspects.
    Reducing diets—Economic aspects.
    Exercise—Economic aspects.
613.712

Cover photograph by iStockphoto
Cover design by Christa Moffitt, Christabella Designs
Internal design by Alicia Freile, Tango Media
Typeset in 10.25/14pt Minion by Alicia Freile, Tango Media

CONTENTS

INTRODUCTION

There's a popular saying that you can never be too rich or too thin. And while it's far better to focus on getting lean and healthy rather than just getting thin, there's no doubt that health and wealth are two fairly popular pursuits.

Yet we are getting fatter and poorer by the day. We are slap bang in the middle of a global financial crisis and an obesity epidemic. Most papers, magazines or current affairs programs regularly run stories on how to lose weight or increase your wealth.

But what if there was a common solution? Is it possible to lose weight and save money at the same time? Could an abdominal crunch save us from the credit crunch? Can you get a tight arse by being a tight arse?

Imagine a weight-loss program that could help you save money. That's the philosophy of *The Tight Arse Diet*. It dispels the myth that being healthy costs more. It shows you how to lose weight and improve your health while also having a few extra dollars in your pocket. It can help you get taut from being tight. You could say it's like killing two birds with the one stone (while losing a stone — that's 6 kilograms for readers unfamiliar with imperial measurement).

A lot of the inspiration here comes from my experiences in the health and fitness industry, working as a personal trainer for more than fifteen years. I often debate with people the importance of their health, and that the money they invest can be repaid tenfold. I think the best parent, partner, employee and performer you can be is a fit and healthy one. Many people want to achieve better health and weight loss, but parting with their hard-earned cash to achieve results can sometimes be a different story. That's fair enough in many cases, as people face a wide range of money pressures in today's financial climate. However, what is disturbing is that when people face financial hardship, their weight and health can often suffer. They assume healthy eating costs more, and load up on what can be seen as cheaper junk food. Maybe that's why a higher proportion of overweight and obese people come from people in lower income brackets.

But I'm here to tell you that healthy eating doesn't have to cost more. You don't have to sacrifice your health for your finances. In fact, healthy eating can actually be cheaper — and *The Tight Arse Diet* will show you how.

I also think people can be reluctant to spend money on weight loss because of past failures, mixed messages, and experiences with products or programs that promised so much, but delivered so little. While the age of information has its advantages, it has also caused a great deal of confusion and misinformation. The lure and promises of quick and easy weight loss can also be hard to resist. If you have an abdominal training device, an old exercise machine or a half-empty packet of weight-loss tea sitting in your house, then you'll probably know what I'm talking about.

There seem to be hundreds of ways to lose body fat, and it can be difficult to sort the facts from fiction. I couldn't count the number of times I've heard of people changing the way they eat based on something they have heard or read without questioning the source or the scientific evidence behind such claims. That's why you'll find some mythbusting facts in *The Tight Arse Diet* to help uncover the common fallacies and misconceptions surrounding weight loss. By arming yourself with this knowledge you can focus on strategies that actually work.

Most of the weight-loss tips in this book include references to one or more scientific studies that prove how effective these tips can be. Throughout *The Tight Arse Diet*, you'll find over 30 'Science says' sections. I have seen them work for my personal training and online training clients, and they can work for you too. I often rely on these studies to calculate how many kilojoules and how much cash you can save.

I've also included a section on my top budget superfoods, and which ones allow you to enjoy healthy food while trimming down without blowing your budget. There's strategic advice on both diet and exercise, and you'll even find some recipes based on my budget superfoods. Each tip will show you either how many kilojoules you could save, how much weight you could potentially lose, or how much exercise that equates to. You'll also learn the amount of money you could potentially save over the short and long term.

I hope you find *The Tight Arse Diet* a useful tool in helping you lose body fat, and for saving a little extra money along the way.

My secrets to lasting weight loss

As a personal trainer, I have designed *The Tight Arse Diet* primarily to help you lose weight and gain health. As the title suggests, you will lose some fat off your backside, but also off other areas such as your tummy, hips and thighs. Note that this book is just as much for men as it is for women.

My weight-loss beliefs and methods have evolved after many years of university study, continued learning and that all-important school of hard knocks — experience. As a personal trainer I have worked with models, athletes, celebrities and people who weighed over 170 kilograms. I have lectured for weight-loss programs, trained people over the internet around the world, and written several books on how to lose weight (or body fat as I prefer to call it). What I have learned is there are a handful of proven strategies that help people get results. I've seen them work time and time again. They're simple and effective. They are designed to help you use up more kilojoules, and reduce the amount of kilojoules you take in (without hunger or deprivation). Then you'll be in the best position to burn off the excess kilojoules stored on your body as fat. These strategies and principles are the foundation of all the weight-loss tips in *The Tight Arse Diet*.

The key strategies are:
- Find ways to reduce your kilojoule intake, especially by cutting back on animal fats, junk food, liquid kilojoules and processed carbohydrates.
- There's more to diet than just kilojoules. Eat foods that not only help you lose weight but also promote good health and wellness. Eat plenty of fruits, vegetables, wholegrains and pulses — such as beans and lentils.
- Learn to manage your portion sizes. Portion control allows you to have small treats when you feel the need. Don't go for the all-or-nothing approach and deny yourself the things you enjoy. You simply won't stick to something if you feel deprived.
- Boost your metabolism. Cutting back on your kilojoule intake (dieting) is not enough as it slows down your metabolic rate. You need to offset this effect by increasing your metabolism through physical activity and exercise, or you will end up losing muscle mass and feeling tired.
- Find ways to increase the amount of kilojoules you use, including planned cardiovascular exercise, incidental physical activity and strength training. And remember, exercise has many other benefits above and beyond weight reduction.
- As you get fitter, continue to progress by increasing the intensity, duration and/or frequency of your activities. Try to incorporate

some interval training into your cardiovascular exercise.

- Successful weight loss is about slow weight loss. Be patient and don't expect fast or continual results. Make small changes gradually and progressively. Make changes you can stick to, and give them time to become habits. Once you have mastered a few small changes, make a few more additional changes. That way your weight loss is more likely to be permanent.
- In terms of your results, don't rely solely on the bathroom scales to measure your progress. It's how you look and feel that's important — not just a number. A tape measure is also a good way to track the shedding of body fat, which sometimes doesn't show up on the scales.
- Be positive about healthy food and regular exercise. Don't look upon them as something you have to do or something you're doing at the moment until you go back to how you were. Healthy food and regular exercise need to become an integral part of your life if you want long-term results. You may as well enjoy it.
- Look after your overall health, including sleep and stress management. These factors work in combination with good nutrition and physical activity to keep your metabolism and hormones working for you, not against you.
- Find what motivates you and keeps you on track. Everyone's different, but whether it's cross-training, a gym membership, a training partner, an online personal trainer or simply an email newsletter subscription, find what works for you.

How much weight can you lose?

It's interesting to see how much weight loss a potential lifestyle change can achieve. For example, who would have thought that just getting rid of butter on your bread could reduce your annual fat intake by over 5 kilograms a year (and save you over $30). There are numerous examples such as this throughout the book. However, I will point out that estimating weight loss is not an exact science.

Weight loss by numbers

Please don't worry if I get a bit technical here. I promise you won't need a calculator to read this book. I do think it's important to explain how I've worked out the amount of kilojoules and potential weight loss each lifestyle tip can offer.

Please understand that it's impossible to be 100 per cent accurate when calculating the kilojoule use and weight loss you can expect from each tip. That's simply because everyone is different. I've had to rely on averages or reference figures, including:

1. **80 kilograms** — The average body weight used in calculations of the kilojoule use and potential weight loss from a lifestyle tip is 80 kilograms. To make your own adjustments, add or subtract 10 per cent to the amount of kilojoules used or saved for every 7 kilograms that you are either over or under 80 kilograms. Weight is one of the biggest variables in determining how many kilojoules your body uses. There are also numerous websites with calculator tools to help you work out roughly how many kilojoules you'll burn off during different activities.

2. **6500 kilojoules** — The average person burns off approximately 6500 kilojoules a day at rest. It's actually around 5900 kilojoules for women and 7100 kilojoules for men. We also eat, on average between 8000 and 10,000 kilojoules per day, which is more than most of us need, and explains why nearly two-thirds of adults are overweight or obese.

3. **$174** — The Australian Bureau of Statistics (ABS) Household Expenditure Survey from 2003–04 (the most recent one available at the time of this book going to print) showed that the average Australian household spent 14.7 per cent of their income on food and non-alcoholic drinks. This includes groceries, takeaways, and eating out at restaurants. ABS figures for May 2008 showed that the average gross weekly earnings of a full-time adult worker in Australia are $1183.10. So I have assumed that the average adult Australian spends around $174 a week on food ($1183.10 x 14.7 per cent = $174).

4. **Kilojoules** — Kilojoules are the nationally recognised unit of food energy, so I'll stick with them. If you still work in the old speak, you can convert to calories by dividing any kilojoule amount by 4.2.

5. **38,000 kilojoules** — You need a deficit of approximately 38,000 kilojoules to lose one kilogram of body fat. That's a deficit of over 5000 kilojoules a day if you want to lose 1 kilogram a week. Every tip in *The Tight Arse Diet* is designed to help you either consume fewer kilojoules or burn more off so you can generate a kilojoule deficit. But there's more to it than that. If you wanted to lose 10 kilograms and you

jogged continuously until you burnt off 380,000 kilojoules (which would take more than 5 days), you wouldn't suddenly lose 10 kilograms (see the following paragraph, which explains how your body adjusts its metabolic rate). It's the consistent changes that you make over the long term that will have the most impact.

Maximising your weight loss with *The Tight Arse Diet*

While each tip in this book gives you a guide to potential weight loss, results will vary among individuals. The amount of kilojoules people burn off will vary dramatically depending on age, gender, weight, body composition, fitness and activity levels, stress levels, hormone balance, sleep, metabolic rate and dieting history. Your body makes adjustments in its metabolic rate to maintain balance. For example, as you get fitter, and when you lose weight, your body burns off fewer kilojoules for the same given task. If you apply every single tip in this book, you won't lose 250 kilograms. Otherwise, successful dieters would eventually disappear, and we wouldn't want that.

I also acknowledge some tips will not be suitable or practical for every reader. So to help you get the most out of this book, I've included a table at the end of the book (see the Appendix on page 174) so you can make your own calculations. There's also space for you to note the page numbers of all the tips that are relevant to you.

Why not assemble a dozen or more tips from *The Tight Arse Diet* that, when stacked together, will form your own personal plan for losing body fat? You can then calculate how much weight your own unique program could help you lose, and also see how much money you could save.

Small changes, big results

The final factor — and the one that will ultimately determine your success — is time. This book will give you many examples of how small lifestyle changes can make a big difference over 12 months. By making changes you can stick to, you can take advantage of this powerful force. Make a few changes that you can stick to over time and once they become a habit, adopt a few more additional changes. After a while, the benefits really begin to stack up. A short-term change (such as a strict diet) that causes a drastic drop in your kilojoule intake will shut down your metabolic rate, making it even harder to strip body fat in the future. It just doesn't work. Be patient, don't expect continual change, and have realistic expectations.

How can this book help you save money?

Applying the principles in this book doesn't make you a financial 'tight arse'. Yes, it's a term that's used to describe people who are 'close' with their money. But that's not what this book is really about. Let me state clearly that I am no financial expert and I am not offering financial advice (even if I do confess I was a bit of a tight arse as a struggling student in my university days). But I am passionate about showing you how to lose weight and improve your health without spending a fortune.

In fact, you can actually use the process of losing weight to help you get ahead financially. Research has shown that losing weight is easier when there is money on the line. My hope is that by giving you some ideas to save money, these can be a powerful incentive for you to lose body fat. For each weight-loss tip, you will see how much money you can potentially save on either a daily, weekly or yearly basis.

I will also outline what studies or statistics I have used to make those calculations. To work out your potential savings, I've had to rely on average prices. That's because the price of food and drink can vary dramatically, not only throughout the country but even in the same suburb. These average prices may not match the price that you normally pay for these items. For example, I have calculated the average cost of a glass of wine at $2.30. That's what you'd pay for a $12 bottle of wine, but it's also a lot more than you'd pay for cask wine and a lot less than you'd pay for a glass at a pub, club or restaurant. So if you feel any of my price estimates don't match your circumstances, please substitute with your own calculations: there's room at the end of the book.

How much money can you save?

Would you like to get paid to lose weight? Does somewhere between $1000 and $5000 sound good? How much you save is really up to you, and the number of lifestyle changes you are prepared to make. Even if you only follow a few tips in this book, you could still save over $1000 a year. Why not use a moneybox and put in a few coins every time you make a lifestyle choice that helps you make a saving. You can also use the table (see page 174) in the back of the book to list together five to ten changes you feel are most relevant to you. Then you can get a real idea of how much you could save. The real savings can be made by sticking to these changes over time — the same way that is also the best way to lose weight.

Enjoy the rewards

A key element in weight loss is to celebrate your achievements and reward your successes. Positive reinforcement helps to motivate, and drives you onwards towards achieving your goals. It's important to have something to aim for, especially when you first make changes to your lifestyle. When you lose weight following *The Tight Arse Diet*, your reward will be extra cash, but put a little thought into how you spend it. You could aim for one large reward when you reach a certain target or give yourself lots of smaller bonuses along the way. Another good idea is to choose rewards that further increase your chances of losing body fat, such as new training shoes, online training, exercise equipment or a healthy recipe book. Try not to use food- or alcohol-related rewards, which can undo your good work. As your body adapts to healthy eating and regular exercise, the sense of accomplishment and boosted energy levels will become a reward in itself.

A final word

Not every tip in *The Tight Arse Diet* will suit everybody. There are tips that are more specific to families, while others may be better suited to individuals. But I genuinely believe there are at least a handful of money-saving, kilojoule-burning opportunities for everyone inside *The Tight Arse Diet*. This book should pay for itself in no time at all. Now to the tips.

PART 1
LIFESTYLE TIPS

TAKE HOLIDAYS THAT ARE HEALTHY AND ACTIVE

How will it affect your weight?

While a holiday is a great way to relax and enjoy being with friends and family, it's one of the most challenging times of the year if your goal is to lose weight. It's not unusual for food and alcohol to be the central focus of social celebrations, while the portions and types of food on offer are unlikely to be found at a health farm. If you eat, drink and laze around a pool, you could return home with a little excess baggage. It can also be difficult to maintain your usual patterns of exercise and healthy eating away from your normal surroundings. There may be a tendency to rely on fast food, takeaways and restaurant meals, not to mention the breakfast banquets.

If you are thinking that holidays should be a time for fun and indulgence, I agree with you. But with a small shift in attitude, and in your lifestyle, you can still enjoy yourself without the holiday weight gain. A little physical activity can help you burn off extra kilojoules, suppress your appetite, and even help you deal with any stressful family situations that may arise. You can also prepare healthy foods and reduce your portion sizes so you can taste and enjoy any indulgence on offer.

Science says: Holiday weight gain is small but often permanent

A study reported in the *New England Journal of Medicine* found that most people gain a little weight on their holidays. While some people can put on over 3.5 kilograms, the average weight gain is around half a kilogram (19,000 kilojoules) over the festive holiday season. This may not sound like much, but the concern was the fact that this extra weight hangs around. That weight was not lost again later in the year, so it accumulates over time. That amounts to an extra 5 kilograms every decade. It's known that the average adult gains approximately half a kilogram to 1 kilogram a year. But it is uncertain whether that weight gain occurs at a slow, steady rate throughout the year or just at certain times, such as on holidays. The researchers thought it was important to learn specifically when people gain weight so that preventative strategies could be put in place. The study found that overweight and obese subjects gained the most weight. The researchers also found that subjects who reported doing more physical activity had less holiday weight gain. This would support the fact that increasing physical activity may be an effective method for preventing weight gain during this high-risk time. One way to almost force yourself to be active is to take a camping holiday. The extra kilojoules you'll burn from setting up and packing away your equipment, and the frequent walking to amenities could potentially add up to an extra kilogram of weight loss if you camp regularly.

Practical tips for being healthy and active on your holidays

Here are some practical tips for doing just that.

- Pack your exercise shoes and make it a priority to schedule some planned walking or running into your day.
- Take the attitude that any exercise is better than none. It's much better to reduce your exercise time than to eliminate it.
- Try to plan ahead for any indulgences. If you know you are going to have a big family dinner, have an extra healthy breakfast and lunch and do some extra exercise.
- Plan an active holiday where trekking, skiing, backpacking or sporting activities are an integral part of your getaway.
- Visit the local gym or fitness centre and ask for a free visitor's pass, or book into accommodation that has its own tennis court or gymnasium.
- Focus your entertainment and time with friends and family around non-food-related activities, such as golf, tennis, volleyball or swimming at the local beach, pool or river.
- Make it fun. Be creative and explore your new surroundings by hiring some bikes or canoes, go bushwalking or have an active picnic with a kite or frisbee.
- Pack some exercise equipment that is light and easy to transport, such as a skipping rope or rubber resistance bands.

- Drink plenty of water instead of fruit juice and soft drink, and drink a glass of water between alcoholic beverages.
- Plan ahead and be organised. Don't arrive hungry at a function where you know unhealthy food is going to be on offer. Schedule time for physical activity and food preparation.
- If you really want to indulge, have a small portion. Deprivation doesn't work because you will always feel like you're missing out.
- Don't forget that it is okay to say no. You don't have to eat everything on offer.
- For breakfasts, stick to fruit, toast and cereal, with skim milk to pour on your cereal. Avoid cooked breakfasts with bacon, eggs and sausages.
- For lunch, it shouldn't be hard to find a ham or chicken and salad sandwich with wholegrain bread. You could easily make some sandwiches in the morning and take them with you.
- Dinner is usually the biggest challenge when you are away from home. Try a lean piece of meat or fish on the barbecue accompanied by a salad (with low-kilojoule dressing). If you don't get the chance to prepare your own food, look for takeaways with lean meat and lots of vegetables, such as an Asian-style stir-fry.
- Snacking can be another challenge on holidays. Try to have fruit, low-fat yoghurt, fruit packs and small portions of nuts on hand. Good savoury snacks include rice crackers with salsa, rice crackers with hummus, pretzels, coloured Japanese crackers and low-fat potato chips. Go easy on regular potato chips, cheese and fatty dips.

CHANGES TO HELP YOU WITH YOUR WEIGHT LOSS	KILOJOULES SAVED	POTENTIAL WEIGHT LOSS OVER A YEAR
Take holidays that are healthy and active	19,000 over a year	0.5 kilogram
Going camping	38,000 over a year	1 kilogram

How can it save you money?

There are a few ways you can be active and save money on your holidays. Firstly, by walking everywhere, you can save on fuel or hire car costs. Secondly, you can prepare your own food instead of relying too heavily on takeaways and junk food. I'll assume you can save about $50 a week using these methods. But the big way you can save money on your holiday accommodation expenses is to go camping. There are some amazing caravan parks with camping grounds that have great facilities, such as tennis courts, heated swimming pools and access to the beach or bushwalks. The amount people spend on holidays can vary dramatically, so my figures are only a guide.

MONEY SAVED EACH WEEK	POTENTIAL YEARLY SAVING
Taking holidays that are healthy and active = $50 (approx.)	$200 with 4 weeks' holiday a year
Going camping = $250 (approx.)	$1000

STRESS LESS, RELAX MORE

How will it affect your weight?

Stress can have a dramatic influence on your body shape and your health. If you are unhappy with your job, your relationship, your children, your finances, your relatives, your neighbours or anything else that dominates your thinking and thoughts, it's hard to prioritise your health.

It's a vicious cycle, as stress can make you feel lethargic. This can lead to bad food choices, abandonment of your fitness plan and make it even less likely that you will get enough sleep. In times of stress, hearty comfort food can be hard to resist.

Stress also triggers the release of the hormone cortisol, which can make you feel hungry. This is one of the reasons why stress has such a strong connection with food and mood, and is often referred to as emotional eating, or comfort eating. When some people experience stress from emotions such as sadness, guilt or frustration, it can trigger a 'craving' or a desire to find comfort from food. Eating for comfort is a common behaviour, and the occasional indulgence shouldn't do you any harm. Although the circumstances of and responses to comfort eating will vary from person to person, emotions can trigger eating behaviour that spirals out of control.

On the other hand, relaxation leads to physical and emotional changes that are the complete opposite of stress. It can strengthen your physical and emotional reserves to help cope with future stress. Learning to relax more is a practical way to prevent weight gain from stress-related eating.

Science says: Stress makes you hungry

Food acts as a distraction from stress-related issues but it won't solve the problem. Gaining control over stress is a vital step in managing your kilojoule intake. A study from Rush University Medical Center found that the more stressors a woman reported, the more weight she had gained over 4 years, even after taking into account variables that influence weight, such as diet, exercise, smoking, and age. Another study, reported in the *Journal of Social and Clinical Psychology*, found that it's during times of stress when people find it hard to resist unhealthy temptations. The researchers found that during periods of high stress, the subjects ate less healthy foods, drank more high-caffeine drinks and slept less. Stress appeared to cause a relapse in behaviours that were previously under control. During times of stress, people could only cope with so much, and were particularly vulnerable to a loss of self-control. Alternatively, relaxation can help you lose weight. A study reported in the journal *Preventive Medicine* found that women who meditated and did yoga lost an average of 2.5 kilograms over 2 years compared to those who focused purely on exercise and nutrition. The researchers believed that reducing stress stops cravings for fatty foods and sweets. By learning and practising relaxation techniques as part of a wider lifestyle change program, the study participants had effective tools to manage stress and emotions without resorting to unhealthy eating. I'll use this relaxation study to calculate how much potential weight you could lose later in this chapter.

MYTHBUSTERS

Won't a detox help me lose weight?

Strict dieting can be stressful (and counterproductive), especially if you are relying on willpower and dietary restraint, or if you are doing a type of exercise you are not enjoying. Research has shown that dieters who restrict their energy intake experience greater levels of stress than those who eat normal-sized meals. Strict dieting is not the solution to weight loss. It can also lead to bingeing and feelings of guilt, which can trigger the release of additional stress hormones. If you feel like you're being deprived, you won't stick with it, or if you do, your stress hormones will make it hard for you to get results. Strict diets simply don't work.

Practical tips to help you stress less and relax more

It's not possible to completely eliminate stress, but you can learn to manage and control it, and reduce its harmful effects on your physical and mental health. Stress management involves two distinct and separate strategies, which include preventing stress, and finding ways to relax. Here are some suggestions that may help.

- Awareness is vital in addressing stress. Is emotional eating is an issue for you? If the answer is yes to two or more of the following questions, it would suggest that comfort eating is having an impact on your diet, and it would be wise to take steps to control it.

  __Do you seek out food when you're feeling stressed or upset?

  __Do you eat when you're not physically hungry?

  __Do you eat until you feel uncomfortably full?

  __Do you ever eat alone out of embarrassment because of large portions or type of food consumed?

  __Do you experience feelings of guilt or self-loathing after overeating?

  __Do you eat when you're bored?

  __Have you ever had friends or family show concern over your eating habits?

- If you are aware that emotional eating is an issue for you, try to develop a better understanding of what triggers it. What events and feelings are associated with it, and what are some non-food-related ways to cheer yourself up or relieve stress? These non-food-related activities to relieve stress can include going for a short walk, ringing a friend, listening to some music, reading or gardening.

- If you are vulnerable to emotional eating, avoid having comfort foods such as chocolate, biscuits, cakes, pastries and ice-cream around the house or workplace. If you can stay strong when you go grocery shopping and keep these foods out of your house, you'll be less likely to eat them.

- If you are vulnerable to stress, try not to take on too much at once. Get to know your limits and get better at using the word 'no'.

- Improve your time management and organisational skills, which can help to prevent a stressful crisis and help you to sleep better.

- Take a few minutes each day to turn off the phone and the television and feel yourself unwind. Escape all the noise by giving yourself a few moments of silence, and savour a few moments of quiet time.

- Immerse yourself in a warm bath or spa to help loosen tense muscles and make you feel relaxed. Add scented oils or bath salts to further set the mood. The feeling of cleanliness after washing is also refreshing.

- When you feel stress building up, take a moment to block out everything and focus on your breathing. Deep breathing is a quick, easy, cheap and natural way to help counter the effects of stress. Increasing your oxygen intake through conscious, deeper breathing can help you relax, and increase your energy levels. Take a slow deep breath in through your nose, then out through your mouth, and repeat ten times.
- Go for a light walk to get you away from a stressful environment. It doesn't have to be an exercise walk, more like a quick escape. Short bursts of activity, such as walking or stretching, help to boost your circulation and clear your mind.
- Include mind/body exercise such as yoga, tai chi and pilates in your training schedule. These activities engage your mind and help you relax, getting you to focus on posture, form, breathing and the abdominal core. The slow, controlled movements are generally low impact. Instructional books and DVDs should be available for free at your local library.
- Listening to slow, soothing music can also help you unwind and calm your mood. Find a collection of songs that calm you, and call on them when you need a time out.
- Massage can help to ease stress and muscle tension. To keep things budget friendly, you can do a massage swap with a friend or family member, or even massage yourself.
- Meditation is a very effective method of relaxation and stress-reduction. It lets you take a conscious break from thoughts and distraction, slowing down your heart rate and breathing rate, and relaxing your muscles.

CHANGES TO HELP YOU WITH YOUR WEIGHT LOSS	KILOJOULES SAVED	POTENTIAL WEIGHT LOSS OVER A YEAR
Practising stress management and relaxation techniques regularly	914 over a week	Over 1 kilogram

How can it save you money?

Learning to stress less and relax more can help you to eat less, and crave fewer comfort foods. We know that stress management can help reduce your kilojoule intake by 914 kilojoules a week (around 2.5 kilograms a year, based on research). This amounts to approximately 2 per cent of your weekly total kilojoule intake. I'll calculate your savings based on the fact that you could potentially spend 2 per cent less on the average weekly grocery bill.

MONEY SAVED EACH WEEK	POTENTIAL YEARLY SAVING
Practising stress management and relaxation techniques regularly = $3.48 (approx.)	$181

SACK YOUR CLEANER AND DO YOUR OWN HOUSEWORK VIGOROUSLY

How will it affect your weight?

Doing your own housework is a good way to burn off a few extra kilojoules, while also improving your strength and endurance. It's not as effective as rhythmic, continuous exercise, but it's still a good source of incidental exercise, especially if you do it vigorously. Housework as an exercise ultimately works best if you use it as an addition to your exercise program, rather than a substitute for it. However, some cleaning tasks can burn over 1600 kilojoules an hour, which is more than a moderate walk. Let's look in more detail at the number of kilojoules you'll burn performing some common household duties at a moderate intensity.

HOUSEWORK TASK	KILOJOULES PER HOUR
Sitting (what you burn doing nothing)	600
Ironing	900
Making beds	950
Dusting	950
Hanging clothes out	1000
Vacuuming	1050
Washing windows	1050
Washing the car	1050
Mopping floors	1200
Sweeping/scrubbing	1650

As you can see, housework can help to increase your kilojoule-burning rate. These tasks need to be done regularly, so by scheduling them into your routine, your house, finances and body can all benefit. It worked for the Karate Kid, who learnt his skills waxing cars. It certainly helped the housewives of the 1950s stay trim, where incidental movement and activity levels were equivalent to walking 5 to 7 kilometres a day. There wasn't an obesity epidemic back then. However, the progressive introduction of labour-saving devices changed all that, with elbow grease replaced by convenience. Cut back on some of those labour-saving devices, and burn off the energy yourself instead of paying for it.

Science says: Housework is a good workout

There is solid research to suggest that housework can be classified as moderate exercise. Anything that gets you moving can contribute to improving your health. The current recommendation for physical activity encourages adults to do 30 minutes of moderate-intensity activity on most days, preferably all days, of the week. This level of activity is linked to a reduced risk of heart disease and diabetes, and the prevention of weight gain. However, for weight loss, the recommendation is actually 45 to 60 minutes of moderate-intensity activity each day. To help achieve this, the International Association for the Study of Obesity (of which Australia is a national representative) encourages people to incorporate lifestyle activities such as gardening and household chores. Another study, reported in *Medicine & Science in Sports & Exercise*, said that household chores can be a workout, but it depends on how much vigour the chore-doer puts into it. The 24 study participants ranged widely in their kilojoule-burning rate for a given domestic task, so any potential weight-loss benefits depend on the level of effort of the individual. The researchers believed that most domestic tasks have the potential to offer health benefits if performed for adequate duration, frequency and intensity.

And finally, a University of Exeter study has shown that vacuuming for 30 minutes a week burns up 28,000 kilojoules a year, while doing the laundry for 1 hour and 10 minutes a week burns up around 39,623 kilojoules a year. It seems you can expect to burn off at least a kilogram of fat a year (38,000 kilojoules) by doing 1 hour of vigorous housework each week. When you consider that inactivity is a major contributor to obesity, then a little extra activity in the form of housework will surely be beneficial.

Practical tips to put some 'oomph' into your domestic duties

I won't make a fool out of myself and attempt to give out any cleaning tips. But there are a few things I can advise you on that can make housework more effective for fat burning. Here are some ways to combine housework and exercise.

- Do all your housework continuously, making it last for 30 to 60 minutes. You'll burn off more fat working this way than doing a few minutes here and there.
- Do your housework hard and fast to get your heart pumping quicker; think of it as power cleaning. You'll achieve more and burn more kilojoules in the process. Very important if you want to burn off serious fat.
- A good guide to your intensity is that you should be able to hear yourself breathing, heavily. If you can hear yourself puffing, you're likely to be burning fat.
- Help your body and your budget by hanging out your clothes to dry instead of using an electric dryer. Weather permitting, you will save on your electricity bill and burn extra kilojoules.
- Try to avoid lots of little rests, which is what reduces the effectiveness of housework as an exercise. Once you've finished one task, move quickly onto the next one. Incorporate other exercises into your cleaning workout. For example, you could do five push-ups after every 5 minutes of sweeping, or ten sit-ups after vacuuming each room.
- Listen to your favourite music while doing your housework. Music is thought to activate the same feel-good hormones that food does, so you might enjoy the experience a whole lot more. Play some up-beat tunes that inspire you to want to go hard.
- While performing any housework, draw your stomach towards your spine (you should feel your navel draw inwards). This will support your spine and improve your core stability.
- Housework aside, you can also include washing and waxing your car. Ditch the car wash, save some coin and do it yourself.

CHANGES TO HELP YOU WITH YOUR WEIGHT LOSS	KILOJOULES SAVED	POTENTIAL WEIGHT LOSS OVER A YEAR
Doing 60 minutes of vigorous cleaning once a week	400 over a week	1 kilogram

How can it save you money?

If you don't have a cleaner, then this tip won't save you any money (but at least you'll have a clean house). For the calculations, I have estimated that a cleaner costs $120 a month, however, prices could vary dramatically depending on the size of your house and the specific cleaning tasks required. Make your own calculations if you feel my estimate is irrelevant to you.

MONEY SAVED EACH WEEK	POTENTIAL YEARLY SAVING
Doing 60 minutes of vigorous cleaning once a week = $30 (approx.)	$1560

USE THE INTERNET TO SUPPORT YOUR WEIGHT LOSS

How will it affect your weight?

If you have access to a computer, there are a number of different ways you can use it to help you lose weight. Of course you still need to exercise and eat well, but there are an incredible number of resources available to you, including:
- information, articles and tips
- recipes
- blogs and message boards
- tools, calculators and charts
- exercise demonstrations and training programs
- newsletters
- product, diet, book and supplement reviews.

As you can see, the internet is an amazing tool for weight loss. There are literally millions of websites that have health, fitness, nutritional and weight-loss-related content. Later in this chapter, I'll give you more specific details on each of these categories of information.

Science says: Log on and lose

The *Journal of the American Medical Association* has found that people who use their computers in conjunction with weight-loss programs lose three times more weight than people who don't. The participants had access to a basic internet program and email counselling. Internet behavioural programs were thought to be an ideal alternative to more burdensome clinic programs, and could be used for longer periods of time. Another study, conducted at the University of Vermont, found that an internet-based weight-maintenance program was just as effective as face-to-face programs. The researchers believed that the internet is a viable medium for promoting long-term weight maintenance.

Email support has also shown to have a real impact on results, including behavioural counselling that is computer-automated. A study reported in the *American Journal of Preventive Medicine* found that an email intervention program is an effective way to significantly improve diet and physical activity by helping people move more, sit less, and make healthier food choices. The *Journal of the American Medical Association* also reported on a study where people who use their computers in conjunction with weight-loss programs lost three times more weight compared to people without a computer. Internet-based weight-maintenance programs were said to be just as effective as face-to-face programs, making the internet a viable medium for promoting long-term weight maintenance.

In addition, weight-loss programs with computer-automated guidance have the potential to reach a much larger audience at little or no expense, and have also been shown to help people get results. This could include weekly emails suggesting small, practical, individually tailored goals, such as eating fruit for a snack three times a week, walking for 10 minutes a day at lunchtime, or walking to the shop instead of driving. The *Archives of Internal Medicine* reported on the results of an internet-based weight-loss program where some subjects had access to additional automated weekly emails. Those with computer-automated emails lost significantly more weight after 3 months than a group who also attended an initial orientation but had no further contact.

The subjects in the automated-email group lost an average of 4 kilograms. With all this evidence that the internet can be an effective tool for weight loss, I'll assume that it can help you lose an extra 1 kilogram a year. To achieve at least a 1 kilogram loss, subscribe to email newsletters that send you information and tips on a weekly basis.

MYTHBUSTERS

I read all about this new diet on the internet.
Will it help me lose weight?

With the steady traffic of diets and celebrity fads, it's hard for people to know what direction to take when it comes to losing weight. The desire to take the quick, easy road to weight loss can really set you up for a fall. There is no miracle cure, although internet marketers are very good at telling you what you want to hear. I've heard of coconut diets, chocolate diets, hot dog diets and magical cellulite vanishing pills. It's the classic case of, 'If it sounds too good to be true, it probably is.' That's why it's important that you don't believe everything you read on the internet. To help you separate the facts from the fiction, ask yourself the following questions when evaluating the information on the internet. If you answer yes to any of these, you can start to raise doubts about what's on the screen.

- Are there any promises of fast, miraculous weight loss?
- Are there claims that you can eat whatever you want, or that you don't have to exercise?
- Are there claims that sound too good to be true or claims that have been questioned by respected health experts or organisations?

Trustworthy weight-loss information, diets or programs are typically backed by scientifically proven results and will list where the scientific research came from or where it was published. Also, the diet or program should strike you as an approach you could realistically stick to over the long term.

Practical tips on how to use the internet to help you lose weight

Use these suggestions to help get the most out of your computer and your weight-loss program. Part of the fun is exploring and finding sites that best meet your needs. Happy surfing.

- If you don't have access to the internet at home, you can normally access it for free at your local library. And while you're there, don't forget to take advantage of the wealth of free information available such as exercise DVDs, audio CD self-improvement programs, health and fitness magazines, healthy recipe books and other books about every subject under the sun, including weight loss.
- Information, quizzes, articles and tips are probably the most common websites that can help you lose weight. Type in a topic that you are interested in by using a search engine such as <www.google.com.au>, and let the fun begin. You can find articles on exercise, motivation, food, and even nutritional information on how much fat or how many

kilojoules are in a certain foods. Some sites even allow you to ask questions of trainers or dietitians.
- There are some amazing recipe sites on the internet. Look for low-kilojoule recipes or adjust the ingredients of your favourite recipe to make sure they help you lose weight, not gain it. Some sites even list the fat and kilojoule content of the recipes.
- Blogs and message boards are a great way for you to communicate with others sharing the same journey as yourself. You may even get some tips on what has worked (and hasn't worked) for others. Many health experts also have blogs, where you can respond to their comments or articles. You may have to join or register to these kinds of site, but it's usually free. These can be a great source of motivation and support, and are more personalised than information-based websites.
- You can use tools, calculators and charts in a variety of ways, such as to calculate how many kilojoules you burn during exercise, how many kilojoules you need each day, what your heart rate should be during exercise, or your waist-to-hip ratio. Charts allow you to plot your weight loss visually and monitor your progress. You can also find online journals and food diaries.
- Exercise programs and training demonstrations. Some websites have professionally designed fitness programs to help you run a half marathon, increase your strength, or improve your running speed. As for visual demonstrations, one of the best is <www.youtube.com>. For example, you could do a search for some of the body-weight exercises outlined in this book (push-ups, sit-ups), and watch a video on how to perform them correctly.
- You can subscribe to free email newsletters that will keep you updated and motivated with information, tips, study reviews and success stories. They can range from daily to monthly in their frequency, and may link to further information on other websites.
- Some sites review weight-loss products, exercise equipment, new diets, and even supplements. It can be helpful to get a real-world opinion on something you are thinking of purchasing. You can also go on message boards and submit your own reviews.
- Finally, and although this is not free, there are chargeable services that are a lot cheaper than some gym memberships. You can also use the

services of an online trainer or weight-loss coach who interacts with you via email. The information is tailored to your needs, and you can stay motivated at a fraction of the cost of a normal personal trainer.

CHANGES TO HELP YOU WITH YOUR WEIGHT LOSS	KILOJOULES SAVED	POTENTIAL WEIGHT LOSS OVER A YEAR
Using the internet regularly as a weight-loss tool	400 over a week	1 kilogram

How can it save you money?

Assuming you already have access to the internet, most of these websites are completely free, and there are a few ways that they could save you money. You could read a bad review of a supplement or the exercise machine you were thinking of buying, and save your cash. You could find enough healthy recipes to save you buying a new cookbook. You could find out enough information on a new diet on the web that you don't feel the need to buy the book. Or you could use an internet site for motivation and support instead of joining a weight-loss support group with weekly weigh-ins. The more you use it, the more you could potentially save. Let's assume you'll save at least $2 a week.

MONEY SAVED EACH WEEK	POTENTIAL YEARLY SAVING
Using the internet regularly as a weight-loss tool = $2 (approx.)	$104

GET MORE SLEEP

How will it affect your weight?

There is a very important relationship between sleep and body fat. A lack of sleep can slow down your metabolic rate and reduce your body's capacity to burn kilojoules. Another problem with a lack of sleep is that it makes you feel fatigued and out of sorts, which makes it harder to motivate yourself to exercise or cook healthy meals. In addition, people who are tired get hungry, and then tend to eat more in an attempt to boost their energy levels. Sleeping less also gives you more hours that you are awake, which means more time to eat. It can create a vicious cycle between a lack of sleep and a lack of exercise combined with poor eating habits. People with abnormal sleeping patterns are at a higher risk of obesity, diabetes and cardiovascular disease. On the other hand, sustained, unbroken sleep is an important way to recharge your body and mind, restore hormone balance and help your body function at its best. A good night's sleep plays an important part in helping to fire up your metabolic rate and in losing weight.

Science says:
Sleep more, weigh less

A 2007 study reported in the *Journal of Clinical Sleep Medicine* found that people who sleep for less than 7 hours per night were three times more likely to be obese than those who averaged between 8 and 9 hours' sleep. The researchers thought that the more time a person spends awake, the more time is available for eating. Also, sleep-deprived people were more tired and less likely to exercise. Sleep deprivation is thought to raise levels of ghrelin (the appetite-stimulating hormone), and lower the level of leptin (the hunger-suppressing hormone). Another study, reported in the *Annals of Internal Medicine*, revealed that sleep-deprived people (those who have less than 4 hours of sleep), had a significant increase in both hunger and appetite. On the other hand, people who had between 7 and 8 hours' shut-eye a night were more likely to be slimmer, and generally lived a healthier lifestyle. One final study, reported in the *American Journal of Clinical Nutrition*, found that people who lack sleep consume up to 20 per cent more kilojoules. The researchers theorised that the body is subconsciously trying to make up for lower energy levels.

Isn't it often advised to get up half an hour earlier and exercise?

That's good advice as long as it comes with the disclaimer that you go to bed half an hour earlier. With the demands of work and family life growing all the time, it seems easy to sacrifice a little sleep now and then. But a lack of sleep disrupts our circadian rhythms and plays havoc with our hormones. Our bodies have evolved over many centuries to adjust to predictable patterns of light and darkness, helping our inner clock, or circadian rhythm, dictate when we sleep. Less than a century ago, before electric light, people slept for between 9 and 10 hours a night. Now that our daylight hours have been extended, most people are lucky to average 7 hours' sleep a night. Sleep patterns can also vary considerably from one night to the next, which can put people in a permanent state of low-level jet lag. The hormones released during deep sleep have a strong influence on your appetite, mood, energy levels and immune system. When you're sleep-deprived, you manufacture less of the hormones that tell you when you're full, and more of the hormones that raise your appetite. So while it's good to have the intention to exercise, try not to sacrifice sleep in the process.

Practical tips to get more sleep

Changing well-established sleep habits takes time. Some of the changes may seem easy, while others might seem a little extreme. However, don't turn your sleep routine upside down in one night. Give yourself time and make the changes gradually.

- Go to bed and, even more importantly, get up at the same time every day. Establishing a routine can make a big difference to your sleep quality. Try to avoid sleeping in on weekends.

- Make your preparation for sleep a priority. Have a pre-sleep ritual, such as dimming the lights, having a bath or shower, reading or listening to quiet music. You could even try some deep breathing exercises.
- Make sure your room is dark. Even small amounts of light at night can interfere with sleep quality. Darkness triggers the release of the hormone melatonin, which helps to decrease the amount of time needed to fall asleep, increases the amount of time a person sleeps for, and decreases tiredness during the day.
- Create the right environment for sleep. Make sure your room is free from noise and distractions. You will also sleep better if your room is well ventilated and kept at a cool, comfortable temperature.
- Avoid large, spicy meals, cigarettes, alcohol and caffeine close to bedtime. These can all make it harder to fall asleep or reduce your quality of sleep.
- Be physically active during the day to help you fall asleep at night. Avoid exercise at night if you have trouble falling asleep.
- Napping is beneficial if you are chronically sleep deprived (such as shift workers), but it can interfere with your night-time sleep. Try to avoid napping unless you've had less than 6 hours sleep.
- Avoid sleeping pills. They are not a long-term solution to improving your sleeping habits.
- Learn to reduce thinking and worrying in bed. Find ways to help you unwind and manage your stress. See page 21 for information on how to stress less.

CHANGES TO HELP YOU WITH YOUR WEIGHT LOSS	KILOJOULES SAVED	POTENTIAL WEIGHT LOSS OVER A YEAR
Sleeping for 1 hour extra each night	325 per night	3 kilograms

How can it save you money?

If you can increase the amount of time that you sleep, that means there are fewer hours when you are awake and able to eat. What's more, a person who is well rested is less likely to feel hungry. That can potentially reduce your food bills. Science has proven that people who lack sleep eat up to 15 per cent more kilojoules. We know the average person spends $174 a week on food and drink, so a well rested person could potential save close to $1350 each year. But 15 per cent is more relevant to people who only get 4 hours' sleep a night. I have tried to be more conservative for my calculations, using 5 per cent for each extra hour of sleep.

MONEY SAVED EACH WEEK	POTENTIAL TOTAL YEARLY SAVING
Sleeping for 1 hour extra each night = $8.70 (approx.)	$452.40

TURN OFF YOUR ELECTRIC BLANKET

How will it affect your weight?

If you sleep with an electric blanket, the body will compensate for this extra warmth by burning off fewer kilojoules during sleep. Here's why. Your body constantly uses energy, even while you're sleeping, which it needs to power all the life-giving functions of the body (heart, brain, nervous system, digestion, and so on). The body also uses kilojoules to generate heat and maintain core body temperature. These survival functions are known as your metabolism (basal metabolic rate to be exact), and they burn up around 315 kilojoules an hour, even while you're sleeping. This figure will vary dramatically between individuals, but is an average figure to keep things simple. If you sleep with an electric blanket (or electrically heated waterbed), your body doesn't have to work as hard to maintain your core body temperature. The electric blanket generates the heat for you, slowing down your metabolic rate and preventing your body from burning off as many kilojoules. I have estimated that your body would burn off an extra 10 per cent of kilojoules by not having an electric blanket over the winter months. Another way that overheating can prevent weight loss is that it can disrupt your sleep cycle. Heat loss actually helps your body fall asleep, and allows you to sleep well. If your body can't cool itself effectively, sleep quality can be affected. You may have noticed that on very hot summer nights you don't sleep as well. Electric blankets make you hot and may make it harder for you to go into deep sleep. This can also occur to a lesser extent if you keep your bedroom extremely warm or if you sleep with a heavy doona. Doonas are between three to five times warmer than a blanket. They might seem cosy when you first tuck into bed, but 2 hours later, when your body gets to the temperature that you will stay at for the rest of the night, you may be too hot.

Science says: The cold hard facts about electric blankets

A study conducted at the Centre for Sleep Research at the University of South Australia found that an increase in body temperature from electric blanket use was associated with disrupted sleep. The researchers observed a significant decrease in sleep efficiency between 3.30am and 7.30am, and an increase in the number of waking episodes during sleep associated with higher body temperatures.

MYTHBUSTERS

Doesn't being hot and sweaty help you lose weight?

Sweating doesn't necessarily mean you are burning more fat. Sweat does indicate that your body temperature is on the rise, but that could also occur from high humidity, high temperatures, or even a fever. To burn body fat, you need to increase your metabolic rate, and measures such as breathing rate and heart rate are a much more accurate indicator than sweat. This explains why a sauna can help you lose weight on the scales (temporary water loss), but it won't help you lose body fat.

Practical tips for sleeping without an electric blanket

In general, most sleep scientists believe that a slightly cool room and sleep environment contributes to good sleep. The point where sleep quality is affected by temperature will vary from person to person, but there are practical steps you can take to make a difference.

- Let your body generate the heat to keep you warm. You just need enough insulation to keep it near your body. Use a few blankets instead of a doona. Blankets allow you to peel off layers as you warm up.
- Use flannelette sheets, which tend to have a warmer feel than cotton sheets when you first get into bed.
- If you and your partner have different temperature needs, the heat-seeking partner can dress in warmer nightwear, or the other partner

could put on less nightwear. You can also fold a blanket so it only covers the heat-seeking partner.

• The idea is to be slightly cooler when you go bed. This is not about you being cold, uncomfortable or shivering. Research has actually shown that an electric blanket can be beneficial for sleep if your bedroom is at or below 3°C.

• If you must have an electric blanket, warm up the bed then turn it off before falling asleep.

• In summer, a small fan or ceiling fan can help to keep you cool.

CHANGES TO HELP YOU DEAL WITH YOUR WEIGHT LOSS	KILOJOULES SAVED	POTENTIAL WEIGHT LOSS OVER A YEAR
Not using your electric blanket	252 per night	1 kilogram (based on 5 months)

How can it save you money?

Turning off your electric blanket or using less heating in your bedroom will not only help you sleep better, but it can also help to reduce your electricity bills. I have based the following calculations on the use of an electric blanket at 2 cents per hour for 8 hours a night over the last month of autumn, the 3 winter months, and the first month of spring. If your usage differs significantly from this, there is space to make your own calculations. What I haven't accounted for is the potential additional savings in your food bills. In the same way that sleeping longer may help to reduce your hunger and therefore your food bills, turning off your electric blanket and improving your sleep quality may give you additional savings.

MONEY SAVED EACH WEEK	POTENTIAL TOTAL YEARLY SAVING
Not using your electric blanket = $1.12 (approx.)	$22.40 (based on 5 months)

JOURNAL YOUR EMOTIONS INSTEAD OF BINGEING

How will it affect your weight?

Life deals us many challenges and stresses, which can sometimes result in low self-esteem or emotional states that are hard to deal with. Feelings of exhaustion, guilt, frustration or sadness can trigger eating behaviours that make it difficult to lose weight. It's common for people to use food to preoccupy themselves, or to block out negative emotions. Chronic stress can also trigger an increase in the appetite-stimulating hormone ghrelin. When the going gets tough, the tough get hungry. This is especially so in our junk-food-fuelled environment, where we are faced with temptation at every corner, at every petrol station or vending machine, in every supermarket aisle and even at the checkout. When we use food to help deal with emotional stress, we usually choose types of food that won't help us lose body fat. Let's face it, health is not a priority when you're a little emotional. This can often result in a vicious cycle of weight gain, dieting and binge eating (also called comfort eating), where food becomes both friend and foe. One of the first steps you can take to get out of this vicious cycle is awareness. It's recognising that you can't solve your problems with food, and that food may, in fact, be making your problems worse. Keeping a food diary or journal that records your mood as well as what you eat can help to develop a clearer picture of your eating patterns. It increases your commitment and awareness of healthy eating, and can motivate you to change your behaviour. The goal is to listen to your body and develop a better understanding of when you are hungry, and when you are full. Not only does a food diary help to keep you aware and accountable for what you eat and drink, it has been proven to be an effective tool for weight loss. It allows you to identify patterns and trouble spots in your eating habits, and helps you become more mindful of any little extra treats that may otherwise sneak in. It gives you clues about why, when and where the extra kilojoules are coming from. Even knowing that you need to write it down might make you cut back on or cut out some unhealthy foods. Once you build an awareness of the areas you need to work on, you can then develop strategies to address them.

Science says: Food diaries can double your weight loss

Research has shown that people (unwillingly) underestimate how much food they eat, especially if they are overweight. That's why food diaries can make such a difference, as they help to rein in large portion sizes, distracted eating and emotional eating. A recent study reported in the *American Journal of Preventative Medicine* found that people who kept a daily food diary lost nearly twice as much weight compared to those who did not. Participants were asked to record their daily food intake and their exercise minutes. After 6 months on a high fruit and vegetable healthy eating plan, it was found that the more often a participant kept a food record, the more weight they lost. Those who kept no food records lost about 4 kilograms, while those who kept a diary for 6 days or more each week lost about 8 kilograms. That's a big difference in anyone's book. An additional study, from the University of Pittsburgh, showed that any type of food journalling is better than none. Dieters who simply wrote down the size of each meal (S, M, L, XL) were just as successful at losing weight as those who tracked specific foods and kilojoules counts. Not only has the ongoing recording of when and how much you eat been linked with losing weight, but it also has been associated with maintaining weight loss.

MYTHBUSTERS

Shouldn't I count carbs?

A major study published in the *New England Journal of Medicine* is bad news for advocates of low-carb, high-carb, low-protein and high-protein diets. The study found it didn't matter which of the four diets people followed. As long as you monitor your portions and keep your kilojoule intake down, you can lose weight. All the diets were high in fibre and low in kilojoules and saturated fat. The participants also exercised for at least 90 minutes each week. After 2 years, each participant lost an average of 4 kilograms. The study involved no low-carb meals, no food combining, no miracle soups, no magic pills, and no giving up your favourite foods. Diets that restrict certain foods and make you feel deprived simply don't work. The key to losing weight and keeping it off is moderation, coupled with portion control and regular physical activity. The great thing about this study is that it was over two years. Short-term studies on low-carb, high-protein diets often show good results initially. However, these diets are very hard to stick to over the long term. Fast weight loss generally results in fast weight regain. So the message here is that the most important item to record in your food diary is not carbs or fat grams. It's kilojoules that count.

Practical tips on how to keep a food journal/diary

Food may serve as a distraction from emotional issues, but it won't solve them. Don't wait for the problem to go away or think that food can solve problems. Keeping a food diary, or journalling, is not necessarily everybody's cup of tea, but the process of chronicling what you eat and why can make a difference, even if you do it only for 1 week. Following are some practical tips to show you how to keep a food diary.

- While you will get the best results from a daily food diary, aim for at least 3 days each week, including 2 weekdays and 1 weekend day.
- As for the physical recording method, use whatever suits you best, such as pen and paper, a computer spreadsheet or your BlackBerry.
- Most people find it best to record the details as they go, rather than relying on memory at the end of the day.
- The essential details to record are:
  __The time and/or meal (breakfast, lunch, dinner or snack) when you eat or drink.
  __Exactly what you had (include water and drinks).
  __How much you had. You can indicate the portion size simply with S, M, L, XL.
  __Where relevant, specify how the food was prepared (steamed, baked, fried).
  __Note your mood and how you felt emotionally at that time when you ate.
- You can also use a food diary to focus on motivation, exercise or individual problem areas by including details on any of the following issues:
  __Your goals for the day.
  __The extent of your hunger (rate it from one to ten, with ten being extremely hungry).
  __Where you ate (kitchen, friend's house, restaurant).

__Who you ate it with.
__The kilojoule content.
__The fat, carbohydrate, protein and fibre content of the meal.
__The details of any physical activity during that day.

• After you have kept a food diary for a few days, try to become more aware of the reasons why you eat which aren't related to hunger. When faced with temptation, question yourself if food is really going to solve the problem.

• Examine what, how much and why you eat, and come up with a list of non-food-related ways to deal with your emotions or relieve stress. Some ideas include going for a walk, reading, calling a friend, listening to music, playing with your kids or taking a bath.

• Learn to distinguish between emotional and physical hunger. Try to identify the events and feelings that are associated with your emotional eating.

• Deal with the source of negative emotion, or plan your life to prevent it in the future. Until you tackle the underlying issues that lead you towards emotional eating, sustained fat loss will be very difficult.

• If there are serious emotional issues connected to your eating, it would be wise to seek professional help from a psychologist or weight-loss counsellor.

CHANGES TO HELP YOU WITH YOUR WEIGHT LOSS	KILOJOULES SAVED	POTENTIAL WEIGHT LOSS OVER A YEAR
Keeping a food diary	325 per day	3 kilograms

How can it save you money?

We know that keeping a food diary can help to monitor your portion sizes and double your weight loss. Taking into account the average weekly $174 food spend, keeping a food diary could potentially save hundreds of dollars a year. I've used a 5 per cent reduction for my calculations.

MONEY SAVED EACH WEEK	POTENTIAL TOTAL YEARLY SAVING
Keeping a food diary = $8.70 (approx.)	$452.40

PART 2
EXERCISE TIPS

LIFT WEIGHT TO LOSE WEIGHT (NO GYM MEMBERSHIP REQUIRED)

How will it affect your weight?

Strength training (sometimes called weight training or resistance training) involves adding resistance to your body's natural movements to stimulate muscle strengthening. This resistance can be in the form of your own body weight (see pages 51–56 for the top eight body-weight exercises), a hand-held weight, pin-loaded weights, hydraulic resistance, elastic bands or water. Increasing your muscle strength can help you lose body fat as it helps to maintain muscle tissue when you are reducing your kilojoule intake. When you reduce your kilojoule intake without exercise, the weight you lose is more likely to be from a loss of muscle or water from the body. But by being active, and especially by including strength training in your exercise program, any weight you lose is more likely to be body fat. Stronger muscles burn more kilojoules, which explains why strength training is one of the best ways to boost your metabolic rate. Strength training can also trigger a number of significant and unique changes that can help to improve your hormone balance, and help to accelerate fat loss.

Science says: Weight training has proven weight-loss benefits

Strength training works best as a complement to your cardiovascular exercise, and not as a replacement. If fat loss is your focus, performing cardiovascular exercise at least 5 days a week is still a priority. But making time for strength training can have a positive impact on your level of fat loss. Here's a study that proves my point. *Fitness Management Magazine* conducted a study to examine the role of weight training on fat loss. Two groups of people followed the same diet, and exercised for 30 minutes a day for 8 weeks. However, one group spent the full 30 minutes on cardiovascular exercise, while the second group did 15 minutes of cardio and 15 minutes of strength training. You can see the results in the table.

EXERCISE PROGRAM	TOTAL BODY WEIGHT CHANGE	BODY FAT WEIGHT CHANGE	MUSCLE WEIGHT CHANGE
Cardio exercise only	Lost 1.5 kilograms	Lost 1 kilogram	Lost ½ kilogram
Cardio and strength exercises	Lost 3.5 kilograms	Lost 4.5 kilograms	Gained 1 kilogram

The cardio and strength training group lost more weight (2 kilograms), and significantly more body fat (3.5 kilograms). The cardio only group actually lost a little muscle tissue, so they could possibly have less energy and a less favourable hormonal environment for fat loss. The cardio and strength training group actually gained some muscle weight. This can help make it easier to lose more weight or at least to keep off the weight they had lost. Because more muscle boosts your metabolism, people who do strength training will continue to burn kilojoules at a higher rate after they've finished exercising.

An additional study, reported in the *Journal of Strength and Conditioning Research*, showed that subjects who completed an hour-long strength-training workout burn an average of 400 more kilojoules in the 24 hours afterwards than they do when they don't lift weights. And note that increase in muscle weight doesn't mean the muscles are bigger. They are just firmer and heavier because they store more water and glucose.

And finally, another study found that a group of women who performed strength training two to three times a week for 2 months lost an average of 1.5 kilograms of body fat, and gained close to 1 kilogram of muscle. So you don't need to do strength training every day to get benefits. Based on this evidence, I'll calculate that you only need to do strength training twice a week, and that you'll burn an extra 400 kilojoules afterwards that you wouldn't have otherwise used if you weren't performing strength training.

Won't my muscles get bulky if I do strength training?

The answer is a resounding 'no' — you won't get bulky from strength training. This is the most tragic health and fitness myth of all. Sadly, this misunderstanding discourages many people from doing strength training, and they then miss out on all the wonderful, weight-reducing benefits it can bring.

Admittedly, you do see bodybuilders looking bulky, with veins popping out. And it's easy to understand why an overweight person would want to avoid any exercise that is thought to make them weigh more. But it's important to understand that very few men and even fewer women have the genetic potential to build bulky muscles. Even those who do must put in near full-time dedication to a lifestyle that demands very heavy lifting, adequate sleep, a strict diet regimen, supplementation, and in some cases, injections of various substances (most bodybuilding contestants are not tested for drug use).

Let me start by explaining that strength training isn't just for young men. The people who can benefit most from strength training are women and older people, as they tend to have less muscle.

The type of strength training that works best for weight and fat loss involves light weights and high repetition ranges, helping you to get strong, firm and energised. Your muscles may get denser and firmer (sometimes called 'toned'), but they will not get bigger. Imagine that your muscles are like a pillowcase, and inactive muscles have their pillowcase stuffed with feathers. Stronger muscles have their pillowcase stuffed with lead. The pillowcase is still the same size when stronger, but it's heavier and firmer. That's what happens to your muscles.

Another myth that does the rounds is that when you stop doing strength training, the muscle will turn into fat. Who comes up with these? Absolutely impossible! Muscle and fat are two completely different tissues, and it is physiologically impossible for one to convert to the other. However, if you stop lifting weights, your body won't burn off as many kilojoules. If you don't eat a little less (because you are now doing less exercise), you could store a little extra fat. While it may appear that muscle has turned into fat, the muscle gets flabbier (less toned), and the fat cells get bigger.

Practical tips for starting a strength-training program

Don't be daunted by this wonderful form of exercise. Following are some practical tips and guidelines on how to get started.

- Aim to do strength-training exercises at least 2 days a week, making sure you have at least 1 rest day in between. Your muscles need more time to recover from strength training than they do from moderate-intensity cardiovascular exercise.
- Strength-training exercises are described in terms of repetitions and sets. Repetitions are the specific amount of times you perform an exercise, while a set is one group of repetitions of an exercise. For example, doing three sets of fifteen knee push-ups means you would perform fifteen knee push-ups three times — forty-five push-ups in total.
- Ease yourself gradually into a new strength-training program. Don't perform an exercise to the point where you can't do any more. You should be able to perform at least ten to fifteen repetitions of an exercise when starting out, otherwise it may be a little too hard for you. Perform one set of each exercise when starting out, and build up to two or three over time.
- Expect to get a little sore approximately 24 hours after performing strength training for the first three to five times. This is a normal adaptation to a new type of exercise, and after a while, you won't get sore afterwards.
- After the first 4 to 8 weeks, start to push yourself a little harder, increasing the repetitions, sets and/or difficulty of the exercises. If you do three sets of an exercise with more than 20 repetitions, look for ways to make it harder.
- Continually progress by increasing the repetitions and sets over time. You may need to write down what you have done each time so you have a number to beat in the future.
- Try to minimise your rest between sets and between different exercises to maximise the amount of kilojoules you burn.
- If you intend to perform resistance training and cardiovascular exercise on the same day, do the resistance training first. Studies have shown that this helps you burn a higher ratio of fat as fuel.

- Perform a cardiovascular warm-up for 3 to 5 minutes before doing strength-training exercises. This helps get blood flowing to your muscles and prevents injury.
- Always perform strength-training exercises in a controlled manner, keeping your back straight and abdominals contracted. Good technique is vital.
- Once you begin to feel comfortable with strength training, you might like to create your own circuit. These are popular in some specialist gyms, where you perform cardiovascular activities between strength-training exercises. Try things like fast step-ups, star jumps, jogging on the spot, skipping, a 1-minute fast walk or slow jog, or a short stint on any exercise equipment you might have.
- Perform some light stretching exercises afterwards to prevent soreness. Make sure to target the muscle groups you have trained.
- Unless you are highly motivated, you will eventually get bored repeating the same exercises over and over. Look for ways to add variety by changing the order of exercises, or even getting hold of some dumbbells or rubber resistance bands to give you some different exercises. You could always ask for them as a present for your birthday or at Christmas. You can also exercise in front of the television, or have some music playing to add interest and fun.
- If you have any doubts, consult a personal trainer or exercise specialist. Yes, it may cost you some dollars, but they can provide you specific advice relevant to you and your circumstances.
- If you feel any unusual pain, discomfort or dizziness during strength-training exercises, stop immediately and see your doctor.

The top eight body-weight exercises

If you'd like to enjoy the benefits of strength training, but don't want to pay for a gym membership, then you can always use your body weight as resistance. There are plenty of exercises you can perform with minimal equipment or expense. Following is a description of eight different body-weight exercises, most of which are graded for different levels of strength.

1. PUSH-UPS

BEGINNER LEVEL — KNEE PUSH-UPS
- While kneeling, place your hands out in front of you under your shoulders, and shoulder-width apart.
- With your abdominals contracted (that is, pull your bellybutton back towards your spine), and back straight, bend your arms and slowly lower your body until your chin hits the ground. Don't bend at your hips. If you can't get your chin to the ground at first, go as far as you can and increase as you become stronger.
- Pause briefly and then push back with your arms to the starting position.

INTERMEDIATE LEVEL — STANDARD PUSH-UPS
- Follow the steps for beginner push-ups, but start on your toes, not your knees.

ADVANCED LEVEL — FEET-ELEVATED PUSH-UPS
- Place your toes on a bench or seat.
- Push up with your hands on the ground, abdominals braced and back straight.

ELITE LEVEL — ONE-ARM PUSH-UPS
- Spread your legs wide apart to provide a base of support.
- Place the pushing hand under your chest, and other hand behind your back.
- Rotate your shoulder a little as you lower yourself to maintain balance.

2. SQUATS

BEGINNER LEVEL — BASIC SQUATS
- Have your feet shoulder-width apart, toes forward, heels flat.
- Stick your butt out and bend down like you were going to sit on a chair.
- Lower yourself down until your thighs are parallel to the ground.
- Keep your back straight and push yourself back up to the starting position.

INTERMEDIATE LEVEL — PAUSE SQUATS
- Follow the steps for basic squats, but pause at the bottom for 1 second.
- Push yourself back up, but don't quite straighten your legs, and repeat with minimal rest.

ADVANCED — DEEP SQUATS
- Follow the steps for basic squats, but lower yourself until your butt nearly hits your heels.
- Slowly push yourself back up to the starting position.

ELITE LEVEL — JUMPING SQUATS
- Follow the steps for beginner squats, then jump in the air after lowering.
- When you land, absorb your weight, and repeat with minimal rest.

3. SIT-UPS

BEGINNER LEVEL — BASIC CRUNCHES
- Lie on your back with knees bent and feet flat on the ground.
- Consciously contract your abdominals and lift your shoulders off the ground.
- Lower slowly and don't rest on ground between reps.

ADVANCED LEVEL — DOUBLE CRUNCHES
- Lie on your back with knees bent and feet in the air above your hips.
- Lift your shoulders off the ground while bringing your knees towards you.
- Lower slowly back to the starting position and repeat, with no rest between sets.

4. CALF RAISES

BEGINNER LEVEL — STANDING CALF RAISES
- Stand on the edge of a step or bench on the balls of your feet.
- Raise your heels so you roll onto your toes.
- Lower your heels enough to feel a stretch in your calves for one rep.

INTERMEDIATE LEVEL — PULSE CALF RAISES
- Follow the steps for standing calf raises, but only lower yourself about 1 centimetre.
- Raise yourself to the top again before lowering yourself all the way down for one rep.

ADVANCED LEVEL — SINGLE-LEG CALF RAISES
- Follow the steps for standing calf raises, but balance on your right foot with your left foot resting on the heel of your right foot.
- Complete your reps then swap feet.

5. DIPS

BEGINNER LEVEL — BENCH DIPS, KNEES BENT
- With your back towards a bench or chair, place your hands on the edge of the bench, fingers facing down.
- With feet out in front and knees bent, lower your body with elbows pointing back.

INTERMEDIATE LEVEL — BENCH DIPS, KNEES STRAIGHT
- Same technique as for beginner dips, but keep your legs straight as you lower your body.

ADVANCED LEVEL — BENCH DIPS, FEET ELEVATED
- Position your hands for beginner dips, and place your feet on a bench, box or ball.
- Keep your legs straight, and lower yourself slowly.
- Raise yourself to the initial position.

ELITE LEVEL — BAR DIPS
- Use two parallel bars that are approximately shoulder-width apart and keep your feet off the ground.
- Lower yourself slowly until your shoulders are mildly stretched.
- Straighten your arms and rise up to the starting position.

6. LUNGES

Beginner Level — Stationary Lunges
- Step forward so that your feet are 1 metre apart, and raise the heel of your back foot. This is your starting position.
- Lower your back knee towards the ground. Your front knee should not extend past your toe.
- Push up and back to the starting position for one rep. Swap legs to complete the set.

Intermediate Level — Step-Forward Lunges
- Standing with your feet together, take a big step forward with your right leg.
- Immediately push back up to the starting position for one rep.
- Repeat stepping forward on the right leg for the full rep count, then swap legs to complete the set.

Advanced Level — Elevated Lunges
- Place your back foot on a step or bench, and your other foot on the ground in front of you.
- Lower your back knee towards the ground. Your front knee should not extend past your toe.
- Push up and back to the starting position for one rep. Swap legs to complete the set.

Elite Level — Jumping Lunges
- Step forward on your left leg so that your feet are 1 metre apart, and raise the heel of your right foot so that you are up on your toes.
- Jump up, and while in mid-air, swing your right leg to the front and your left leg to the back.
- When you land, absorb your weight, then repeat with minimal rest.

7. OBLIQUE CRUNCHES

- Lie on your back with knees bent, feet flat on the ground and arms crossed.
- As you lift your shoulders up, rotate your body to one side, touching your elbow on the opposite thigh.
- Return to the starting position and don't rest on the ground. Alternate sides.

8. BRIDGE UPS

- Lie on your back with your knees bent, feet flat on the ground, and arms folded across your chest.
- Keeping your shoulders on the floor, slowly lift your butt off the floor, pushing up so that your back is completely straight, forming 'the bridge' between your feet and your shoulders.
- Squeeze your gluteal muscles (the big ones on your butt) as you come up.
- Go halfway down without letting your butt touch the floor then bring your butt up again. Repeat.

CHANGES TO HELP YOU WITH YOUR WEIGHT LOSS	KILOJOULES SAVED	POTENTIAL WEIGHT LOSS OVER A YEAR
Performing strength-training exercises twice a week	800 a week	1 kilogram

How can it save you money?

Body-weight strength-training exercises are completely free, requiring little more than a towel and a glass of water. That can save you considerably on an annual gym membership, which can cost anywhere between $700 and $1500. I've based my calculations on an average fee of $1100 per year. If this doesn't match your gym fees, you can make your own calculations.

MONEY SAVED EACH WEEK	POTENTIAL YEARLY SAVING
Performing body-weight strength-training exercises twice a week = $21.15 (approx.)	$1100

SET UP A HOME GYM AND DISCOVER WAYS TO USE THE EXERCISE EQUIPMENT YOU ALREADY OWN

How will it affect your weight?

Home gym equipment can be a helpful weight-loss tool or a worthless dust collector, depending on how often and how effectively you use it. Exercising on home fitness equipment is great if you don't like gyms, can't afford a gym membership, have to stay at home caring for children or other family members, or if you don't like exercising outdoors. It can also be a good complement to your existing exercise program (such as walking), either as a variation, or an alternative on cold, wet or windy days when you don't feel like going outside.

Another important consideration is that embarrassment has been identified as one of the major barriers that prevent people from starting an exercise program. Fitness equipment allows you to start at a comfortable level in the privacy of your own home. A home gym doesn't have to be expensive or elaborate to be effective. It can be as simple as a bit of empty floor space that allows you to do body-weight exercises (see the previous tip for more details). The amount and type of equipment you accumulate will depend on your budget, your floor space and your goals.

Science says: Home exercise equipment can increase weight loss

A study reported in *Annals of Behavioral Medicine* found that people with a home exercise machine were 73 per cent more likely to start exercising. Another study, published in the *Journal of the American Medical Association*, found that overweight women who used home exercise equipment (a treadmill) as part of their exercise regimen lost twice as much weight as their peers who did not have that option but were instructed to do the same amount of walking. In a 12-month period, women with treadmills lost 2.5 kilograms more weight (5 kilograms versus 2.5 kilograms) compared to women without the equipment. I will use this figure in my calculations later in this tip. It came as no surprise that participants with treadmills maintained a higher level of exercise throughout the study. The researchers stated that the equipment made the activity easier to adopt because it allowed people more flexibility in their exercise regimen, including the ability to exercise in the rain or the dark. It was also thought the treadmills acted as a visual reminder of exercise, and that they helped people accumulate short sessions of activity.

MYTHBUSTERS

Aren't all exercise machines the same?

Not at all. A study reported in the *Journal of the American Medical Association* compared the energy-burning potential of different exercise machines, and found the treadmill was the most efficient of six types tested, including stair climbers, rowers and exercise bikes. The subjects exercised at a perceived level of exertion estimated as 'somewhat hard', and within a training range of 60 to 90 per cent of their maximum heart rate. The results showed that for what was perceived as the same level of effort, the treadmill used the most energy. The treadmill burned 40 per cent more energy per hour than the least effective machine, the stationary bicycle. This is because your body uses much fewer muscles when your weight is supported by a bike seat. The table details the kilojoules used per hour at a 'somewhat strong' intensity on each of the machines tested.

EXERCISE MACHINE	KILOJOULES BURNED PER HOUR
Treadmill	2950
Stepper	2625
Rower	2535
Cross-country ski machine	2590
Cycle with moving handles	2130
Stationary bike	2084

Practical tips for setting up your home gym

Because *The Tight Arse Diet* is all about maximum results for minimum expense, this section will focus on some budget-friendly home gym equipment. When you consider that a lot of people don't end up using their home gym equipment after a few months, it makes sense to start off with a small investment. Once you have established a good routine, and feel like you are motivated to continue, you can then spend a little extra and expand your range. Following is a list of some of the best home gym resources and ideas to help you get you the most mileage for your money.

- **A fitball** — You can pick these up for between $20 and $40 and they are very versatile. Do a search on the internet, or buy a book that outlines the wide range of exercises you can perform.

- **Rubber resistance bands** — Rubber tubes, sheaths and bars with rubber straps attached can be used to provide resistance for a wide variety of strength-training exercises. They are light, easy to use, easy to pack away, and you can even take them with you on holidays.

- **Dumbbells** — Dumbbells allow for a large variety of exercises and don't take up too much space. You can get pre-moulded dumbbells or an adjustable set that allows you to increase the weight as you get stronger.

- **A skipping rope** — Skipping is a great way to incorporate some high-intensity activity into your day. You can have fun, get fit, burn fat and kilojoules, prevent osteoporosis and reduce your risk of heart disease all at the same time. It's a cheap activity you can do almost anywhere, with the flexibility to make it harder or easier depending on your fitness level.

- **A pedometer** — Pedometers are inexpensive, usually costing between $15 and $45. They can measure your incidental movement around the house, and give you a guide to how active you have been that day.

- **An exercise mat** — A mat with good cushioning can make your workout safer and more comfortable. Most mats roll up easily for convenient storage.

- **Exercise videos and DVDs** — These are a great indoor option, especially those that target aerobic fitness and weight loss. Look for videos from qualified instructors rather than popular celebrities, and programs that include different levels catering to a wider audience. You might even be able to borrow one from a friend to find what you like

- **Punching bag and boxing gloves** — Boxing gives you a great upper-body workout, not to mention the energy boost and stress relief from hitting something. Incorporating kickboxing moves and leg movements such as squats, jumps and kicks with boxing will use more muscles, and give you an even better fat-burning workout. You should be able to get these items for under $100.

- **A heart-rate monitor** — These devices with a watch and chest strap start at around $40, and help to make sure that your intensity during exercise is ideal for fat burning. They can give you a motivational boost, and some models even beep at you if you're not working hard enough or if you're pushing yourself too hard.

- **A mini trampoline** — These start at around $50, and they are a comfortable exercise option that are easy on your joints. It's basically a formal way to run on the spot, but you can add dumbbells to increase the intensity. They work best as part of a circuit as you may get bored spending too much time on one.

- **Get creative** — Do your own indoor circuit by alternating a series of strength-training exercises (push-ups, sit-ups, lunges, dips, squats) with short bursts of cardiovascular exercises. The cardio could include fast step-ups (use a doorstep or a bottom stair and step from the floor to the stair; alternate the foot you lead with), skipping, star jumps (go from a crouch to a jump; throw your arms and feet wide so your body is like an X at the top of the jump), knee tuck jumps (from a standing start, jump straight up, tucking your knees towards your chest; bend your knees as you land) or jogging on the spot. Do each exercise for 30 to 60 seconds then repeat.

- **Try before you buy** — If you want to purchase a more expensive piece of equipment, but aren't sure how much you'll use it, consider hiring it for a few months. It's a good way to see how much value you would get out of the machine at a fraction of the cost. Some companies even have a hire/buy scheme, where the rental price comes off the purchase price should you decide you wish to own it. Some people also just hire equipment in the colder months. Look up exercise equipment in your local Yellow Pages to see if there is a supplier near you.

- **A little pre-love** — Another good way to expand on the variety of machines in your busy home gym and save a few extra dollars is to look for second-hand exercise equipment. There's never a shortage of treadmills, bikes and other machines on eBay, in the trading post, your local paper or at local garage sales.

Practical tips on how to use the equipment you already have

The actual act of buying exercise equipment won't help you lose weight, but it will help you build exercise into your lifestyle. The best equipment for fat burning is a cardiovascular-based exercise machine like a treadmill, bike, elliptical trainer, stepper or rowing machine. If you already have one of these machines at home, or are contemplating getting one, here are some tips on how to get the most out of them.

- Read the instruction manual and take advantage of all the variable programs and uses a machine has to offer. Subtle variations in the way you use machines allows you to work the body in a different way. Some examples include skipping sideways at a slow treadmill speed, using a stepper without holding on, going backwards on an elliptical trainer, or standing while pedalling on a stationary bike.

- One way to increase the likelihood of using your equipment is to work out with a friend or family member. You'll find more details on training with an exercise buddy on page 61.

- To add to the enjoyment of exercise on a cardiovascular machine like a treadmill or exercise bike, watch television, listen to music or have the radio on. This helps to make the time go by quicker, and keeps you motivated. Another idea is to go harder during the commercial breaks, which is known as interval training.

- Most cardiovascular exercise machines are ideal for interval training because you have a timer right there in front of you to measure your sprints and rests. For example, you can push yourself really hard for 20 seconds, then take it slow for 20 seconds to catch your breath.

- Use feedback from the machines display, such as the speed, distance travelled, time, intensity/wattage, RPM and calories/kilojoules. This allows you to set benchmarks and gives you targets with personal best times or distances to beat. You can also use the kilojoule counter to let you know when you've burnt off an indulgence.

- Set yourself mini goals and challenges to keep you motivated, such as training for an event, or exercising for 21 days in a row. By testing your boundaries, you can expand your horizons and push yourself beyond your comfort zone.

- If you own a treadmill, be aware that the gradient has a dramatic influence over the effectiveness of your workout. A higher incline forces your body to work harder against gravity, using more muscles and burning more kilojoules. Because there is no wind resistance on a treadmill, use an incline of at least 2 per cent to compensate.
- Another treadmill tip is to avoid holding on to the handrails, which alters your body's natural movement patterns and has a negative impact on your knees or back. While you might need the handrails occasionally for balance, swinging your arms also helps to maximise the effectiveness of your treadmill workout, increasing the aerobic benefit and kilojoules used.

CHANGES TO HELP YOU WITH YOUR WEIGHT LOSS	KILOJOULES SAVED	POTENTIAL WEIGHT LOSS OVER A YEAR
Investing $100 and set up your own home gym	1800 a week	2.5 kilograms
Using the exercise equipment you already own	1800 a week	2.5 kilograms

How can it save you money?

According to a recent survey from the International Health, Racquet and Sports Association, 67 per cent of gym members also own home exercise equipment. By actually using the equipment you have, you could save over $1000 a year on gym membership. I've estimated gym membership costs $1100, the same as my previous tip on lifting your own body weight. I've also estimated that you can set up your own home gym for around $100, including a fitball, exercise mat, rubber resistance band and skipping rope. If these estimates don't match your circumstances, you can make your own calculations.

MONEY SAVED EACH WEEK	POTENTIAL YEARLY SAVING
Investing $100 and set up your own home gym = $19.23 (approx.)	$1000
Using the exercise equipment you already own = $21.15 (approx.)	$1100

EXERCISE WITH A FRIEND OR PARTNER

How will it affect your weight?

Lifestyle changes are harder to achieve by yourself, so why not rally a little support for your cause. Friends and family members with a similar health or weight-loss goal can be a great source of motivation and encouragement. When you make a commitment to exercise with someone else, you're more likely to stay committed. It can push you to train more often and skip fewer sessions, and above all, it can make exercise more fun. It makes the time go faster having someone to talk with, and gives you the opportunity to share your thoughts. It's more rewarding when you both work towards something and achieve it together. A training partner can fill a similar role to a personal trainer, they can make you work a little harder than you normally would on your own, just as you can stretch and challenge them in return. They can play tennis with you, spot you at the gym, or increase the safety of your evening walks. They might even introduce you to new activities that you might not have considered before, or that you can't do on your own. You can check up on each other, motivate each other, and dramatically increase your chances of success. It can make a big difference to have someone depending on you on those days when you don't feel like training.

Science says: Exercise with a training partner makes a dramatic difference

A study reported in the journal *Preventative Medicine* found that women's overall activity was positively related to support from their friends and family. The more social support a person receives, the better the weight-loss results. And according to further research, reported in the *American Journal of Health Studies*, you'll be more likely to stay on track by having a training partner. After examining the drop-out rates at gyms, researchers found that only 6 per cent of couples who joined together gave up within 12 months compared to

43 per cent of people who were in a relationship, but who joined alone. In other words, having a training partner made you six times more likely to still be exercising after 12 months due to that extra support, which improves feelings of control and confidence. By joining forces, you can help each other train more, eat better, and stay positive about lifestyle changes. Based on this evidence, I'll assume you can lose an extra 2 kilograms of body fat each year by taking advantage of partner power and finding and exercise buddy.

MYTHBUSTERS

My parents are overweight, so I am destined to be overweight too.

People often like to blame their weight problems on genetics. And although there are some rare exceptions, lifestyle is the more likely cause. While genes load the gun, it's the environment that pulls the trigger. Excess body fat has only become significant health problem in the last 30 to 40 years. It's not possible for genetics and human evolution to change so much in such a short period of time. That time period happens to coincide with massive changes to our lifestyle. Technology has made us more reliant on labour-saving devices, while our diet has become more dependent on processed foods and food prepared away from home. Regardless of your genes, if you're not eating more kilojoules than you burn, then you're not likely to gain weight. Of further interest is research that looks at excess weight as not so much an issue of genetics, but rather as socially contagious. A study reported in the *New England Journal of Medicine* found that your chances of becoming obese are much higher if someone you are closely connected to becomes obese. According to the study, if someone you consider a friend becomes obese, your chances of becoming obese increased by 57 per cent. The impact of your spouse or sibling becoming obese on your health was also significant. The research suggests that as people get bigger, they come to think that it is okay to be bigger because those around them are bigger. The researchers also found that even friends of friends in social networks can have an impact. However, there was also a positive to come out of this research. It suggested that thinness was also socially contagious. Working together with one person to lose weight can potentially help several others.

It's another reason why people who join to exercise together tend to have better results than those going solo. And another reason why exercising with a friend or partner can help you lose weight.

Practical tips for exercising with a friend or partner

Working with friend or partner on the road to weight loss and wellness can make the journey a whole lot easier. Here are some practical tips to help you find the right person, and what you can do to maximise your chances of getting results.

- Look towards your partner, relatives, kids, friends, neighbour or co-workers to be your training partner. Ideally, find someone with similar goals and comparable fitness levels.
- Important attributes to look for in a training partner include punctuality, consistency, a positive attitude, honesty, discipline, lives nearby, is open minded to try new exercises, and is enthusiastic and fun to be around.
- Once you've found a training partner, make a plan of the training you intend to do together on a weekly basis, and set aside a time and place. Write it down in your diaries, just like you do for other important appointments, meetings or events. You don't have to do something together every day, but having a plan and being organised will help turn intention into action.
- Don't get too competitive with your training partner (unless that works for you). The real person to compete against is yourself.
- Talk to each other about the things that normally hold you back from exercising more. Try to identify any barriers, and come up with solutions that the two of you can work on together.
- Give yourselves an incentive for sticking with your plan for a set period of time. If you've had a good month, reward yourselves with a massage or trip to the movies. You can even work towards greater rewards when you achieve your goals, such as a holiday. Just avoid food-based rewards that undo all your hard work.
- If your immediate partner is a little reluctant to start exercising, don't nag or humiliate them. Just start doing it yourself, and show them that it is possible to make healthy changes. You won't motivate your partner to exercise more by lying on the couch and using their lack of enthusiasm as an excuse. Make improvements to your own eating and exercise habits first, and set a good example.

- Go for a short walk with your partner at night to unwind instead of planting yourselves in front of the television.
- Dogs make great exercise companions because they are constant in their daily need to be walked, they don't need time to get ready and they never have an excuse not to exercise. They can also add to your safety if you like to walk in the early morning or late evening.
- If you have trouble finding the right person, why not start up a walking group in your area. Make up some flyers and pin up some notices. It's a great way to boost motivation and get to know the people in your area.

CHANGES TO HELP YOU WITH YOUR WEIGHT LOSS	KILOJOULES SAVED	POTENTIAL WEIGHT LOSS OVER A YEAR
Getting a training partner instead of joining the gym	1460 over a week	2 kilograms

How can it save you money?

Finding your own training partner can potentially save you money on gym fees or help you get better value out of a gym membership. When you consider that an annual gym membership can cost anywhere between $700 and $1500, that's a considerable saving. It can also save you the cost of hiring a personal trainer, or reduce the amount of sessions you have each week. As a personal trainer I see the difference that it can make in terms of motivation, guidance and results. But it can be expensive choice if you're on a budget. An average personal training session can cost anywhere between $50 and $100, or a minimum of $2500 a year if you have at least one session a week.

It's a little hard to come up with an exact figure for this tip, but I'll base my calculations on a saving of $1100 a year: the average price of a gym membership. If you don't have a gym membership or a personal trainer, then this tip won't save you any money, but it can help you lose weight.

MONEY SAVED EACH WEEK	POTENTIAL TOTAL YEARLY SAVING
Getting a training partner instead of joining the gym = $21.15 (approx.)	$1100

GET INTO GARDENING, GROW YOUR OWN VEGETABLES

How will it affect your weight?

We know that even moderate-intensity exercise can increase your body's metabolic rate and help you burn more kilojoules. Gardening is a great example of a moderate-intensity activity that you may not even think of as exercise. But moderate gardening burns over 600 kilojoules in 30 minutes, which is a higher rate than golf. It provides a wide variety of movements that will work and improve your agility, flexibility, cardiovascular fitness and muscle strength. The more muscles involved in your activity, the more kilojoules you'll burn. You can turn your garden into your own personal fitness centre by combining a range of vigorous and active movements such as digging, raking, pulling weeds, walking and squatting. This will give you a good, whole-body workout. While not a direct substitute for cardiovascular exercise, it is a great addition to your exercise routine. Fortunately, there's wide variety of tasks associated with gardening to keep things interesting. You can always find something different to do throughout the day, and throughout the different seasons. To help maximise the impact that gardening can have on your body shape, why not channel your efforts into creating a thriving herb and vegetable garden. Having your own fresh herbs and vegetables will really encourage you to eat more plant foods, which in turn will help reduce your kilojoule intake. Not only will a herb and veggie garden reduce your grocery bill, it will add a fresh, fat-free flavour to all your healthy recipes.

Science says: Some toil in the soil is good exercise

Research conducted at the Kansas State University in the United States has found that gardening is an effective way to exercise, and offers similar health benefits to walking. Subjects had their heart rate, oxygen intake and energy expenditure measured while they pushed a mower, dug holes, pulled weeds and carried soil. By comparing the heart rate elevations caused by gardening with those caused by exercising on the treadmill, the researchers determined that gardening could be classified as moderate-intensity exercise. Moderate-intensity exercise is physical activity that causes an increase in breathing or heart rate, and allows your body to burn kilojoules at a faster rate. In a further boost for weight loss, a 2002 study showed that regular gardeners have lower blood sugar levels, which can reduce the release of the fat-storing hormone insulin. It can help your kids stay active as well. A 2003 study showed that non-competitive activities like gardening lure children away from a sedentary lifestyle, and just 30 minutes of gardening a week made them more likely to eat vegetables. There are also health benefits associated with gardening that go above and beyond weight loss. Gardening can help you meet the physical activity guidelines for Australians, which is to participate in at least 30 minutes of moderate-intensity physical activity on most days of the week in order to maintain and improve optimal health. A study conducted at the University of Arkansas also found that strenuous yardwork (pushing a lawn mower, pulling weeds) had the same beneficial effect on bone density as weight training. So gardening can play a role in helping to prevent osteoporosis.

MYTHBUSTERS

Do vegetarians find it easier to lose weight?

There is a general perception that being a vegetarian makes it easier to lose weight and research supports this theory. A recent study reported in the *Journal of Human Nutrition and Dietetics* found that people who converted to a vegetarian diet reduced their kilojoule intake by over 800 kilojoules a day. After 6 months, they had reductions in their waist and hip measurements and their level of body fat. But other studies have shown that it really depends on what type of vegetarian you are. For example, vegetarians can still get a lot of kilojoules and fat from large portions or from milk, butter, cream, cheese, vegetable oil and yoghurt. This was demonstrated by a study reported in the *International Journal of Obesity* that divided subjects into four groups, including meat-eaters, fish-eaters, egg-and-dairy vegetarians, and vegans (who eat no animal products). The meat-eaters had the highest body mass index (BMI), which is an indicator of being overweight. Fish-eaters and egg-and-dairy vegetarians had similar, moderate BMI levels, while vegans had the lowest. The difference in weight among these groups relates to the difference in kilojoule intake. Fish-eaters and egg-and-dairy vegetarians ate approximately 4 per cent fewer kilojoules than the meat-eaters, while the vegans had over 14 per cent less. This supports my inclusion of eggs and seafood as budget superfoods, while others I have included such as oats, potatoes, pulses and vegetable-based soups are vegan staples. While you may not want to go the extremes of being a vegan, filling up on more vegetables, fruits, wholegrains and pulses should help you to reduce your kilojoule intake and level of body fat. This eating style, even with moderate amounts of low-fat dairy, fish, eggs, lean meat, and small portions of nuts and plant fats, will be lower in kilojoules than a diet with large amounts of fatty meats and full-fat dairy products.

Practical tips for gardening and growing your own vegetables

Gardening is a wonderful way to be active while enjoying the great outdoors and keeping your surroundings looking good. It also helps to reduce stress and gives you a sense of accomplishment. By following the tips to create your own vegetable garden, you'll soon have the unique satisfaction that comes with using home-grown herbs and vegetables in your meals.

- Begin with light activities (pruning, picking up fallen branches) to warm up, then pick up the pace and treat your gardening like a workout.
- Because gardening is a stop-start activity, it needs to be carried out for a long duration to help assist fat burning. Don't expect 5 minutes of pruning to transform your body. Try to keep at it for at least 30 minutes at a time, and do so at an energetic pace that gets you breathing at a faster rate. It is also ideal if you are able to garden at least 3 days a week.
- Look after your back by bending with good posture, and alternating your dominant hands on tools to get a balanced and back friendly workout.
- For your vegetable garden, try to find a space that gets more than half a day's sun. Start with herbs and vegetables that are easy to grow, like

parsley, mint, chives, green onions, green beans, tomato, rosemary, lettuce, spinach and bok choy.

- Try to have more vegetarian meals in your diet. We know that eating more vegetables will help you lose weight. Learn to grow vegetables you like eating and fit with the recipes you love.
- Science has proven that eating a wide variety of foods increases your exposure to different nutrients. This can also help you to lose weight (as long as you don't eat more kilojoules in total), because your metabolism functions at its best when all your nutritional needs are met. If you have the space, grow a wide variety of herbs and vegetables of different colours and textures to increase the variety of foods and nutrients in your diet.
- If you live in an apartment you can still grow herbs in pots on the balcony or windowsill. You can also hook up with someone else to grow your own vegetables, or find out if there is a community garden in your area.
- One disadvantage of gardening is the seasonality, and the reduced amount of activity required in winter. Make sure you do a little extra exercise such as walking if you are gardening a little less.
- Get to know what grows well in your garden and climate of your area through trial and error. As your gardening skills develop, you can also learn about complementary planting, and seek out additional plants that reduce the need for fertilisers and insecticides.
- The cheapest way to start is with packets of seeds, although you can pick up some seedlings at minimal cost.
- Use your food scraps and garden waste to make your own compost heap. Over time, this can fertilise your vegetable garden for free.
- Get your children working in the garden. Encourage their interest by letting them plant some seeds or seedlings. Get their heart rate up with raking and weeding.
- One of the most common gardening tasks that people pay for is to have their lawns mowed. By doing it yourself, you can save money, and burn lots of kilojoules in the process. Think of how many kilojoules you could burn with an old-fashioned manual mower.

CHANGES TO HELP YOU WITH YOUR WEIGHT LOSS	KILOJOULES SAVED	POTENTIAL WEIGHT LOSS OVER A YEAR
30 minutes of gardening three times a week	1800 over a week	2 kilograms

How can it save you money?

If you currently pay someone to mow your lawns or maintain your gardens, you can make immediate savings by doing it yourself. In addition, growing your own vegetables and herbs can save you money off your food bill. For example, a bunch of herbs will cost you $2 at the supermarket, yet you can buy a seedling for around the same price, and within weeks, you'll have your own ongoing supply. The last household expenditure survey showed that fruit and vegetables made up 13.7 per cent of the total food and grocery bill. Based on today's figures, that's around $24 a week. After factoring in the cost of seeds, seedlings and fertiliser, let's assume your vegetable garden can save you $5 a week. This could be considerably more or considerably less depending on the size of your garden. I've also assumed that you would garden for an average of 30 minutes, three times a week. This could be a little more in the warmer months, and a little less in the cooler months.

MONEY SAVED EACH WEEK	POTENTIAL TOTAL YEARLY SAVING
30 minutes of gardening three times a week = $5 (approx.)	$260

WALK INSTEAD OF DRIVING

How will it affect your weight?

I've written a whole book on this subject (*Walk Off Weight*), and I am very passionate about it. If you had to pick one activity that is ideal for weight loss, and suits the majority of people, walking is a clear stand-out. There really is no cheaper, easier and more enjoyable way to burn off kilojoules and body fat. All you need is some comfortable clothes and a suitable pair of shoes. Because walking is an aerobic activity, it's great for weight and fat loss. 'Aerobic' means 'with air', so your body uses oxygen (and with it fat) as an energy source. Yet the amount of kilojoules you'll burn depends on how hard and fast you walk, and how long you walk for.

To help you lose weight, I want to differentiate between two types of walking. They are:

• **Planned walking**

This is a scheduled, organised, constant walk for 30 to 60 minutes. Walking is a great way to lose body fat. But walking is a very easy, efficient activity for your body, and there are some important strategies you'll need to incorporate into your training if you want to get serious weight-reducing results. I have outlined these strategies in the practical tips later in this chapter.

• **Incidental walking**

Incidental walking is the short bits of activity you accumulate over the course of the day, such as walking from the car to work, to the bank or around the house. This type of walking doesn't have to involve breaking into a sweat, puffing or needing a shower immediately afterwards. The reduction in incidental movement is one of the leading contributors to the increasing rates of obesity around the developed world.

Beyond the weight-loss benefits of walking, it can also reduce stress and boost your energy levels. Being a low-impact exercise (walkers always have at least one foot on the ground), there is only a small chance of injury. It also means there is no pain or discomfort.

Science says: Cars are fattening

Car usage in Australia increased by 20 per cent in the decade between 1981 and 1991. This has also coincided with an increase in the rate of people who are overweight or obese. Using a car denies you the chance to be physically active, and will have a big impact on your body shape. A NSW health survey investigated the body weight and activity levels of workers using different modes of transport. They found that people who drove to work were more likely to carry excess weight compared to people using other modes of transport such as walking, cycling and public transport. And the more often they drove to work the greater their weight. Additional research from the *American Journal of Preventive Medicine* found that people who live in neighbourhoods where they must drive to get anywhere are significantly more likely to be obese than those who can easily walk to their destinations. Each hour spent in a car was associated with a 6 per cent increase in the likelihood of obesity and each kilometre walked per day reduced those odds by nearly 5 per cent.

MYTHBUSTERS

Isn't running better than walking for weight loss?

There are some advantages to running over walking, which include:
- Running burns three times more kilojoules than walking.
- Running has a bigger impact on boosting your metabolism.
- You get a better workout in less time.
- Running gives you a quicker path to fat and weight loss.
- If you can walk fast, you should be able to run.
- Little bursts of running adds intensity to your walks.
- You are more likely to get a 'runner's high'.

But the debate about whether you should walk or run ultimately comes back to the individual because it depends upon your weight and level of fitness. If you are walking fast for over 1 hour without much duress, running may well be better than walking. However, if you weigh over 100 kilograms, have existing knee problems, are fairly unfit, and don't have shoes with excellent cushioning, running may be too stressful on your joints. A recent study comparing the weight-loss effects of running and walking found that, for people who hadn't exercised in a number of years, it didn't matter what they did. Both the runners and walkers lost weight, although the runners did lose slightly more (0.68 kilograms). It seems running is a better option for advanced walkers, not beginners.

Practical tips to include more incidental walking in your day

While planned walking is a much better fat burner, there are still significant benefits to be had from just walking more in everyday life. And by doing more incidental walking instead of using your car, you can save considerable amounts of money. Here are some ways to incorporate more incidental movement into your day.

- Whatever your mode of transport to work; aim to include some walking as part of your journey. For example, if you catch public transport, get off several stops before your destination. A small backpack would allow you to carry a change of shoes and a water bottle if needed.
- If you are short on time, incorporate a few short bouts of walking into your day. While four 10-minute walks aren't quite as effective as one 40-minute walk, it's a lot better doing that than doing zero minutes' walking.
- If you get the opportunity, take the stairs instead of the escalator or elevator.
- When parking your car, pick a distant spot in the parking lot so you get to walk a little further. You probably won't have too much trouble finding a space.
- If you walk at night, be safe. Wear light-coloured or reflective clothing, walk facing oncoming traffic, walk in well-lit, populated areas and try to use a footpath. If you have any concerns, try to walk with a friend or partner.
- If you are wearing an mp3 player, keep the volume at a level where you can still hear car noise and traffic.

Practical tips for burning more fat during your planned walks

Walking is the most popular form of exercise in Australia. Here's how to make sure you don't just stroll aimlessly, but you walk off weight.

• **Walk fast**

Speed matters. People who maintain a faster pace while walking will burn more kilojoules, and get better results. After a few weeks of regular walking, a leisurely stroll just won't cut it anymore. If you can't hear your breath while you walk, you're not walking fast enough. Hearing yourself puff lightly is good sign you're burning fat.

• **Include intervals**

So many people walk at the same, steady pace, day after day, walk after walk. Little random bursts of effort at different intensities really boosts the kilojoule-burning, fat-burning and fitness-increasing benefits of walking.

• **Head for the hills**

Hills are a walker's best friend. They help you increase the intensity of your walks without having to go fast or rely on running. Actively seek out hills and power up them. Stairs are another great way to add intensity.

• **Swing your arms**

A pronounced, purposeful swinging will burn extra kilojoules (up to 10 per cent more) and help you generate more speed. Keep your elbows bent to a 90 degree angle, keeping your shoulders down and relaxed.

• **Add variety**

Try to vary the location, time of day, intensity and duration of your walks to maintain interest. Look for ways to add variety to your walking routine, such as entering an event or fun run or going for a bushwalk. This helps to keep your mind fresh and prevents boredom.

• **Continue to progress**

It's also important to push yourself a little faster as you get fitter. Set out a special personal-best course over a given distance, and try to beat your best time every week or two. You can even use gadgets like a heart rate monitor or pedometer to give you feedback.

• **Walk before breakfast**

A walk before breakfast helps to burn a higher proportion of fat as fuel. Research has shown that up to 50 per cent more fat is burned (although the number of kilojoules burned was the same) compared to people doing an identical amount of exercise after breakfast.

CHANGES TO HELP YOU WITH YOUR WEIGHT LOSS	KILOJOULES SAVED	POTENTIAL WEIGHT LOSS OVER A YEAR
Walking 10 kilometres a week instead of driving	2000 over a week	3 kilograms

How can it save you money?

Walking can be done almost anywhere, anytime, by anyone — and, best of all, it's free. The amount of money you can save will vary dramatically, depending on how much you walk, how often you substitute car use with walking, the current price of petrol and your reliance on transport. But no matter how much you walk instead of drive, there are significant savings to be made by reducing your dependency on a car. And it's not just petrol savings. You can also factor in oil, depreciation, and wear and tear on the car. In Australian capital cities, some 30 per cent of all car trips are less than 3 kilometres, and half are under 5 kilometres. Some of these trips could easily made by walking. The Australian Conservation Foundation estimates that walking 10 kilometres a week instead of driving saves the average family $900 a year (not to mention the reduction in greenhouse gas emissions). But for the calculations, I have used the trusty tax department's more conservative estimate of 66 cents per kilometre for a medium car (1601 to 2600cc). They also estimate the cost at 55 cents for a small car (1600cc and below), and 67 cents per kilometre for a large one (over 2600cc), so you can always make your own calculations, depending on the type of car you drive.

MONEY SAVED EACH WEEK	POTENTIAL TOTAL YEARLY SAVING
Walking 10 kilometres a week instead of driving = $6.60 (approx.)	$343

GET ON YOUR BIKE AND RIDE

How will it affect your weight?

Cycling is a great outdoor addition to your exercise program for burning fat and aerobic conditioning. Although cycling is not quite as effective as running or walking for fat loss because your weight is supported by the seat, you can still burn off a significant amount of kilojoules. Cycling can strengthen and tone the muscles in your legs and butt, and because cycling is non-weight bearing, it is very kind on your joints. Cycling can add variety to your exercise routine, and allows you to see so much more than you would while walking or running. The fresh air in your face and the rhythm you can get into is addictive. Mountain biking is also popular, and while a little more extreme, is one of the most enjoyable ways to burn off kilojoules. For every hour of cycling, you'll burn around 1200 to 1700 kilojoules depending on the gradient and speed that you ride.

Science says: Cycling (especially with intervals) is a great fat burner

A recent study conducted at the University of New South Wales compared two groups of overweight women. Using a stationary bike, one group cycled at a steady, constant state for 40 minutes. The other group cycled for 20 minutes but performed frequent, intense 8-second bursts followed by 12 seconds of active rest, where they pedalled at a very slow speed. The interval-training group lost three times more weight than the steady-state cyclists. That's triple the weight loss in half the time. Training at a higher level of intensity (in small, tolerable doses) helps your body adapt to a higher level of fitness and stamina. Intense exercise triggers a bigger boost in your metabolic rate, so you will continue to burn kilojoules at a higher rate after you have finished training. So cycling does help you burn kilojoules and fat, but the message to come out of this study is to include interval training whenever you can. What's more, cycling to work can be a real lifesaver. A 14-year Danish study with over 30,000 subjects found that those who rode to work had a 39 per cent lower death rate compared to people who drove.

*If intervals and interval training is so good,
shouldn't I do them all the time?*

If you are overweight or have a history of heart disease, don't push your-self too hard too soon. Make your interval training only slightly harder than normal, with short intervals and long rest periods. Do not attempt interval training at near-maximal effort until you have developed a good base level of fitness over 2 to 3 months. Over this time, gradually increase the level of intensity, increase the duration of the intense interval phase and shorten the rest phase. It's also important to realise that as your train-ing gets more intense, your body needs more time to recover. It's best to plan out your training over the week so your interval training days are interspersed with lighter and longer training days in between. Aim to per-form interval training two to three times a week, and more regular steady-state training — where you work out at a lower intensity for a longer duration — two to three times a week. Check with your doctor if you have any concerns.

Practical tips on how to use your bike instead of driving

Do you have a bike at home collecting dust? It could be making a big difference to your budget and your backside. You don't need a lot of fancy gear to get started. Here are a few tips on using your bike more instead of driving.

- Safety is a major priority for cyclists, especially if you are on a busy road. Follow traffic laws — always wear a helmet. Wear bright colours and reflectors, and ride like the drivers don't see you. Make sure you have a light if you ride at night and always be on the lookout for parked cars with opening doors.
- If you are worried about getting sweaty, plan ahead. Consider where you can have a shower at your destination, and take a change of clothes in a backpack or keep some at work. Look for solutions, not excuses.
- Use your water bottle frequently along the way. Taking regular, small sips is the best way to keep yourself hydrated. You could even consider

a hydration backpack if your rides last longer than 1 hour.
- Be warned: carrying around a portable pump and a repair kit with a spare inner tube is a lot less hassle than having to walk your bike home.
- Try to include some intervals during your rides. To apply this practically (where you can't constantly look at a timer on an exercise bike), you can use random landmarks to indicate the starting point for your intervals and rests. Try to use things like a driveway, cross street, parked car or telegraph pole to mark where you start and (further down the road) stop your intervals.
- You can also use hills as a type of forced interval. Really power up a hill, and then pedal slowly to catch your breath at the top.
- A computerised display can be a good accessory, allowing you to monitor your current speed, average speed, distance covered, duration of journey and kilojoules used.
- Other accessories that you might find add enjoyment to your riding experience include bike-riding glasses, gloves, toe straps and a gel padded seat if you find your bike seat uncomfortable.
- To give yourself an instant exercise bike, you can get a device called a 'trainer' that supports the back wheel of your bicycle and allows you to use it indoors.

CHANGES TO HELP YOU WITH YOUR WEIGHT LOSS	KILOJOULES SAVED	POTENTIAL WEIGHT LOSS OVER A YEAR
Riding 20 kilometres a week instead of driving (60 minutes of cycling at a modest pace)	1700 over a week	2 kilograms

How can it save you money?

According to the Australian Bureau of Statistics Household Expenditure Survey (2003–04), transport currently makes up 16 per cent of the average Australian family's budget, which is on a par with both housing and food costs. With the price of petrol sky-rocketing in recent years, commuting with your bike can save you some serious cash (and benefit the environment). While walking instead of driving may be helpful for very short trips, using a bike gives you an alternative for longer journeys. During peak hour in some cities, it can be quicker to cycle than it is to drive. Huge savings can also be made by becoming a one-car family (and a forced way to cycle or walk more). If you take into account the cost of insurance, registration, depreciation, maintenance and fuel, it's estimated you could be $8000 to $10,000 better off each year. Even after factoring in the additional planning required, some minor inconveniences and extra public transport costs, you would still be a long way ahead. For the calculations, I have used the same figures as the 'walk instead of drive' tip on page 76.

MONEY SAVED EACH WEEK	POTENTIAL TOTAL YEARLY SAVING
Riding 20 kilometres (60 minutes of cycling at a modest pace) = $13.20 (approx.)	$686.40

WATCH LESS TELEVISION

How will it affect your weight?

Time spent watching television has a strong association with excess body fat because as your viewing hours increase, so do your chances of being overweight. Watching television is a sedentary activity. It not only influences what you eat, but where and how much you eat as well. Following is a list of some of the reasons why watching television can increase stored body fat.

- It decreases the time you have available for planned physical activity.
- It decreases the time you have for planning and preparing healthy meals.
- It is an inactive use of your leisure time.
- It slows down your metabolic rate.
- It can increase your kilojoule intake because of the convenience of nibbling and snacking while viewing.
- People often eat poor-quality food in front of the television, which may be related to the influence of junk-food advertising.
- Portion sizes may be higher, as the distraction of television causes people to overeat.

If you are serious about reducing stored body fat, there are much better ways to use your time instead of watching television. One of the main excuses people give for not exercising is they don't enough time, yet many people watch several hours of television each day. Time spent in front of the television is inactive time, time that could be used for exercising, or at least doing incidental movement.

Science says: The more you watch, the more you weigh

Several surveys have found that people who watch large amounts of television (3 to 5 hours per day) are fatter than those who watch less. Researchers from the University of Massachusetts found that people who watched television during a meal consumed an average of 1200 more kilojoules than those who didn't. It's believed that watching something on the screen distracts you, and keeps your brain from recognising that you're full. Another study showed that women who watch more than 3 hours a day were found to be twice as likely to be obese than those who watched less than 1 hour a day. Additional studies have shown that the metabolic rate of children who watch television is comparably lower than in those are at who are at rest or reading. It appears that television can have a 'trance-like' effect on the body, which lowers the metabolic-, or kilojoule-burning, rate to lower than baseline levels. The average person burns off approximately 275 kilojoules per hour, so by not watching television, your body could potentially use an extra 5 to 10 kilojoules in that hour, even if you just sit and read. Better still, imagine if you used that time to exercise.

Practical tips for watching less television

Television might seem like a great way to unwind, but at what price to your health? Rather than cutting out television, why not try cutting back? Here are a few ideas on just how to do that.

- Limit the amount of time you watch television, videos and DVDs to a set duration, such as 30, 60 or 90 minutes each day.
- Limit the amount of time you spend playing television, video and computer games.
- Only watch the programs you really want to watch.
- Cut back on snacking and eating while watching television.
- If you do snack while watching television, make sure the food is healthy.
- Increase your incidental activity by hiding the TV remote control and get up every time you'd like to change the channel.
- Get active while you watch television by doing floor exercises, preparing a healthy meal or using an exercise machine.
- Do something during the ad breaks, such as household chores or moving about.
- Tape shows and fast-forward the advertisements to reduce the time you spend in front of the television.
- Have television-free nights on 1 to 2 days each week.

How can it save you money?

The primary monetary saving from watching less television is the reduction in electricity use — which, admittedly, is modest. There is also the potential to save on food costs by eliminating distracted eating and larger portion sizes. Who knows, your television set might also take longer to break down. According to the organisers of Earth Hour, watching 1 hour of television on a 42-inch plasma screen costs approximately 5 cents. I have used this figure to make the money-saving calculations. If you have a bigger or smaller television or you wish to cut back on more or less than 1 hour of television watching a day, there is room for you to make your own calculations.

CHANGES TO HELP YOU WITH YOUR WEIGHT LOSS	KILOJOULES SAVED	POTENTIAL WEIGHT LOSS OVER A YEAR
Watching 1 less hour of television per day	At least 10 per day or 520 a year	Less than 1 kilogram

MONEY SAVED EACH WEEK	POTENTIAL TOTAL YEARLY SAVING
Watching 1 less hour of television per day = 35 cents (approx.)	$18.25

SWIM LAPS AT AN OCEAN OR HARBOUR POOL

How will it affect your weight?

Swimming is a good exercise for improving your cardiovascular fitness and muscle tone, but there are some doubts about its ability to help you lose weight. I've heard it said that it's better to walk around a pool than to swim in it if you want to lose weight. That's because:

- The water supports your weight, so fewer kilojoules are needed to help you move.
- Fat floats, so the fatter you are, the more you float, and the fewer kilojoules you will use in water.
- Women naturally have a higher proportion of fat to muscle, and a lower centre of gravity than men. Women actually float better in water, so they use fewer kilojoules than men.
- Maintaining normal body temperature is much easier during and after swimming than during land-based activities. This reduces the exercise-induced boost of your metabolic rate, and reduces the appetite-suppressing effects of exercise. In fact, it's not uncommon to feel ravenous after swimming.

If you like swimming, don't worry — it's still a good exercise. Ultimately, the best type of exercise is the one you enjoy because it's the exercise you will be most likely to stick to over the long term. After all, swimming still burns kilojoules, and while it may not be quite as effective as walking or running, it's still better than watching television.

Unfortunately, there are no additional weight-loss benefits from swimming in an ocean or harbour pool compared to swimming in an Olympic-sized pool. This tip is kilojoule- and weight-loss neutral, unless you combine your ocean pool swim with a walk.

Science asks: Is swimming slimming?

A study from 1987 compared the effects of swimming, stationary cycling and walking in overweight women. The study participants did 1 hour of exercise daily for 6 months. The researchers found that the weight of the walkers and cyclists decreased by 12 per cent but there was no change for the swimmers. This well-publicised study led people to conclude that swimming was not effective for weight loss. However, the study failed to look at diet, attendance, exercise intensity or whole-body composition (fat loss versus weight loss), and has since been criticised as being too simplistic. More recent studies that have looked at the effects of swimming on body composition have shown mixed results, however it is generally considered that swimming is slightly less effective than land-based or weight-supported activities for weight control. However, there are steps you can take to make swimming more effective for fat loss.

Practical tips for making swimming more effective for weight loss

There are steps you can take to maximise the fat burning and weight reducing benefits of swimming. These include:

• **Include intervals**

One of the main disadvantages of swimming for weight loss is the reduced amount of kilojoules that you use compared to weight-bearing, land-based activities. However, interval training can help to overcome this problem. Interval training uses structured bursts of high-intensity effort followed by recovery periods to dramatically boost the kilojoule-burning, fat-burning and fitness-increasing benefits of swimming.

• **Kick hard**

Improving the quality of your stroke can make a massive difference to your performance and enjoyment of swimming. To help maximise your speed and kilojoule use during freestyle, try to turn your feet into flippers. Keep your legs taut and your feet flexible, and use a scissor-type movement, which helps to utilise the powerful gluteal muscles.

• **Continually challenge yourself**

Try to set yourself a personal challenge every week or two. Get your competitive juices flowing and put yourself in race mode by competing against the clock. Set a distance, time or lap challenge that fits in with your schedule, and your training goals. For example, if you have 20 minutes, see how many laps you can complete in that time. Then, try to make this your regular personal-best swim, and continually strive to beat your best effort.

• Do some additional exercise out of water

If your goal is weight loss, don't rely on swimming alone as your only form of exercise. By all means, incorporate swimming into your exercise program, but look to include additional weight-bearing exercises that are ideal for fat burning, such as fast walking or slow jogging.

• Try other water-based exercises

Swimming is not the only water-based exercise you can use to lose weight. As long as you move vigorously against the resistance of the water, you can still burn a considerable number of kilojoules. Why not try shallow-water walking, deep-water running, kick-boarding or aquarobics?

• Manage your appetite after swimming

Swimming is associated with a greater stimulus of your appetite compared to land-based activities. Don't undo all your hard work with an uncontrollable urge to eat. So be aware and drink plenty of water after swimming, which can rehydrate you and prevent any food cravings.

CHANGES TO HELP YOU WITH YOUR WEIGHT LOSS	KILOJOULES SAVED	POTENTIAL WEIGHT LOSS OVER A YEAR
Swimming in an ocean/harbour pool instead of an Olympic pool	neutral	neutral

How can it save you money?

If you are lucky enough to have easy access to an ocean pool or harbour pool, then this tip can save you money. These ocean and harbour pools are usually free, compared to Olympic pools, which charge on average $4 a visit. If you don't live near the beach but want to save a few dollars, you might be able to find a lake, river or dam. The calculations are based on three swims a week through the warmer months of October through to March. If this average price or the duration of the swimming season doesn't match your circumstances, there is room to make your own calculations.

MONEY SAVED EACH WEEK	POTENTIAL TOTAL YEARLY SAVING
$12 (approx.)	$288

TAKE THE KIDS TO THE PARK INSTEAD OF THE MOVIES

How will it affect your weight?

One great way to get active is to get the whole family involved. A supportive family environment can make all the difference when it comes to losing weight and exercising more. Take the initiative and include your children as part of your weekly exercise program. Exercising together as a family is a great way to strengthen family bonds and relationships. A trip to your local park creates the perfect opportunity for both parents and kids to be active together. And when you're at the park, don't just sit there and watch your kids burn off kilojoules. Get involved. The activities you incorporate into your park time are limited only by your imagination. If your children are younger, the emphasis should be on activity and movement — not exercise. At the very least, you can all have fun while doing some incidental activity. And you'll burn a lot more kilojoules playing in a park for 2 hours than you would sitting idle in a cinema seat.

Science says: Be a healthy role model

The Australian Sports Commission believes parents have a significant role to play in encouraging involvement in sport and physical activity. The provision of some yard space for play, along with simple, inexpensive play equipment, parents can consciously create a culture of physical activity in the family home. People look towards one another for what is an acceptable weight. By being an active parent, you can set the pattern for your whole family. Be the one among your family and friends who makes physical activity socially contagious.

Practical tips for making the most out of visiting the park

Activities and games give you the chance to have fun and interact with your family in the great outdoors. Here are some tips on making sure your next visit to the park is fun.

- Try to walk or ride bikes to get to the park (if it's practical).
- Shake out your picnic blanket and make the most of your local park or grassland. Don't forget the sunscreen and a healthy lunch.
- Search out books and websites on children's games and activities for the outdoors.
- Play movement-based activities such as tag, hide-and-seek, hopscotch or jumping rope, which can be great for burning calories and improving fitness.
- Be as active as you can around the playground, and join in the fun. If your children are happily playing with other kids, find your own space to do some body-weight exercises.
- Some activity ideas include kite flying, frisbee, volleyball, badminton, tee ball, soccer, bike riding, cricket and rollerblading.
- Go for a family bushwalk through a national park or just trek through some local bushland. It costs next to nothing and you can choose the terrain to suit all ages and levels of fitness. Make sure to wear good-quality footwear, and pack plenty of water and healthy snacks.
- If you live near the ocean, take a family trip to the beach. There's something for everyone, and most activities require little or no equipment. Beyond just swimming and walking on the sand, you could try bodysurfing, bodyboarding, beach volleyball or swimming laps in the ocean pool.
- If you don't live near the beach, visit your local pool. Swimming can be a source of fun as well as excellent physical activity.
- Depending on the age of your kids and your budget, why not try some adventure activities such as mountain biking, paddling or indoor rock climbing.

CHANGES TO HELP YOU WITH YOUR WEIGHT LOSS	EXTRA KILOJOULES USED	POTENTIAL WEIGHT LOSS OVER A YEAR
Taking your kids to the park instead of the movies	1100 per person and 6600 over a year	1/6 of a kilogram

How can it save you money?

It doesn't cost you a thing to go to the park, and there is the added benefit of actually talking and playing with your children. What's more, you get to be active at the same time. Even better is that when you avoid the cinema, you won't get pestered into buying all that junk food. The following calculations are based on figures from the Motion Picture Distributors Association of Australia, which estimates the average price for a family of four to see a movie is $44.68. I have calculated the annual saving based on attending the cinema six times a year instead of twelve. If these average prices or attendance rates don't suit your circumstances, there is room to make your own calculations.

MONEY SAVED	POTENTIAL TOTAL YEARLY SAVING
Taking your kids to the park instead of the movies = $44.68 (approx.)	$268.08

PART 3
FOOD TIPS

DRINK LESS
ALCOHOL

How will it affect your weight?

Cutting back on your consumption of alcohol will certainly help you to lose weight and remove stored body fat. Alcohol is fattening for a few reasons. Alcohol itself cannot be stored in the body (alcoholics are usually thin), but it delays the use of food as a fuel source, making your food more likely to be stored. Alcohol and drinks containing alcohol are very high in kilojoules. The concentrated kilojoules in alcohol become a priority fuel source for your body, and your body begins to focus on burning off the alcohol rather than the food you eat. This is even more of a problem when you think of the foods that are normally consumed with alcoholic drinks, such as beer (pies, hot dogs, nuts, chips) and wine (cheese, crackers, dips). These foods are generally high in fat, and are much more likely to be stored when combined with alcohol. Alcohol also increases the release of insulin (a fat-storing hormone), especially in combination with sugar-based spirit mixers, such as soft drink and fruit juice.

CHANGES TO HELP YOU WITH YOUR WEIGHT LOSS	KILOJOULES SAVED	POTENTIAL WEIGHT LOSS OVER A YEAR
1 less drink per week	400 over a week	0.5 kilogram
6 less drinks a week (similar to 1 less bottle of wine or 1 less six-pack of beer)	2400 over a week	3 kilograms

Science says: Alcohol causes a metabolic meltdown

Alcohol is a depressant to your central nervous system and slows down your metabolic rate. Studies have shown that alcohol can cause a temporary decrease — up to 33 per cent — in the amount of fat the body burns. One study, published in the *Journal of Nutrition*, found that drinking alcohol has a strong influence on the accumulation of abdominal fat. Abdominal fat is a known risk factor for cardiovascular diseases. The study found that in both men and women, the more drinks consumed per drinking day, the higher the abdominal fat measurement. They also found that it's not just the total amount that you drink each week that's important, but also the way that you drink it. Binge drinkers (more than three to four drinks per drinking session) had more abdominal fat than people who consumed the same amount of alcohol but consumed small amounts on a regular basis.

MYTHBUSTERS

Isn't red wine good for you?

The suggestion that red wine is good for your health often interferes with the message that alcohol is fattening. While the antioxidants in red wine are beneficial for cardiovascular health, the same benefits can be found from eating fruit and vegetables. Moderate amounts of red wine may reduce heart-disease risk in some people, but all types of alcohol are fattening. Any alcohol in moderation still increases your appetite and reduces your willpower to say no to unhealthy foods.

Practical tips for reducing your alcohol intake

Cutting back on alcohol may be a challenge for some, while others might see it as an easy step. Have a look at the practical tips and see if there are realistic ways you could cut back on your kilojoule intake from alcohol. It might be easier than you think.

- Whatever amount of alcohol you currently drink, reduce it.
- Aim to include 3 to 5 alcohol-free days (and nights) each week.
- Try to avoid consuming alcoholic drinks together with fatty foods. Look for healthier food choices to combine with alcohol, such as low-fat potato chips, vegetables (dip them in salsa or cottage cheese), vegetable-based dips (salsa, low-fat hummus, baba ganoush), low-fat crackers, air-popped popcorn (no butter), and pretzels.

- If you do consume fatty foods with alcohol, try to keep your portion sizes small.
- Choose lower kilojoule drinks such as light beers, spirits with diet mixers or wine and soda.
- Try to reduce the portion size of your lunch or dinner if you are drinking alcohol at the same time. This can help to compensate for the extra kilojoules from the alcohol.
- Try to be active on the days you drink alcohol.
- When you consume alcoholic beverages, try spacing out each drink with a glass of water in between.
- Add ice to drinks like wine, alcoholic cider and extra ice to spirit-based drinks to water them down. A little ice can also be refreshing in the warmer months.
- Don't binge drink, which is consuming more than three drinks a day for women, and more than four drinks a day for men.
- If you do indulge in binge drinking, be aware that alcohol in excess can lead to inactivity and excessive fat cravings the next day. If you wake up a little dusty, try to make sure you stick to a healthy breakfast and avoid greasy foods.

How can it save you money?

The average adult Australian spends approximately $35.49 a week on alcohol, or $1846 a year (Australian Bureau of Statistics 2008). The amount of alcohol you cut back on will determine how much money you save. The amount you save will also depend upon where and what you normally drink.

You would expect that the alcohol you drink at home would be cheaper than drinks consumed at commercial premises. In terms of the type of alcohol you drink, there is also a price difference depending on the quality and quantity of alcohol. For example, low-alcohol beer is generally cheaper than full-strength beer. To calculate the average price of a drink, we know that the average Australian adult consumes 10 litres of pure alcohol a year (Australian Bureau of Statistics). If a standard drink contains 12.5ml of alcohol, then the average Australian consumes 800 standard drinks a year (fifteen a week). So the average price we pay for a drink is $2.30 ($1846 ÷ 800). I have also averaged out the amount of kilojoules per standard drink.

MONEY SAVED EACH WEEK	POTENTIAL TOTAL YEARLY SAVING
1 less drink per week = $2.30 (approx.)	$120
6 less drinks per week = $13.80 (approx.)	$718

CHANGE THE WAY YOU DRINK TEA OR COFFEE

How will it affect your weight?

Tea and coffee can have both a positive and a negative impact on your weight. The caffeine in tea and coffee has no fat and virtually no kilojoules. But the major problem with tea and coffee is the company that it keeps, including:

• **In the drink**

When you start to add sugar, milk and even cream to your cup of tea or coffee, the kilojoule and fat content escalates.

• **With the drink**

The foods that often accompany tea and coffee are high in kilojoules and fat, such as biscuits, donuts, cakes, pastries and desserts. It may also be hard to eat small portions of these foods with your tea or coffee because caffeine is a stimulant and can stimulate your appetite. There is some research to suggest that people who drink coffee tend to have more fat in their diet.

• **Associated behaviour**

Coffee and, to a lesser extent, tea are associated with behaviours known to cause weight gain, like sleeplessness and stress.

What's more, caffeine can have a negative impact on your hormone balance. Caffeine is known to reduce your sensitivity to insulin, so the body releases more of this fat-storing hormone. When you consume tea or coffee with fatty foods, which is often the case, the extra insulin dramatically increases the chances that the dietary fat in those foods will be stored as body fat.

Science says: Instead of a biscuit, have a workout with your coffee

The caffeine in tea and coffee will actually help you to burn more fat during exercise. A study reported in the *Journal of Medicine and Science in Sports* found that consuming caffeine (in the form of black coffee) 1 hour before exercise made a significant difference to fat use. The caffeine-consuming athletes used an amazing 107 per cent more fat as fuel compared to those on a placebo. This is because caffeine encourages the muscles to use fat as fuel earlier, instead of using up our limited supply of glycogen. Also known as the 'glycogen-sparing' effect, this is why caffeine also allows you to exercise for longer. In fact, the caffeine-consuming athletes in this study delayed their time to exhaustion by 19 per cent compared to the placebo group. The caffeine group also rated their perception of effort as much less, indicating that exercise felt easier. The amount of coffee consumed for this study was 4 to 5 mg caffeine per kilogram of body weight, or roughly two cups of black unsweetened coffee. Higher dosages did not increase benefits, and it was shown that they may even be detrimental. Some secondary benefits to consuming caffeine before exercise included stronger muscle contractions and improved tolerance to pain and fatigue. With less pain, you're able to work out longer and harder, burning more fat and improving your performance. Studies have also shown that caffeine can help reduce the post-workout soreness that discourages some people from exercising. Research published in the *Journal of Pain* found that two cups of black coffee cut post-workout muscle pain by up to 48 per cent. When you take all this scientific research into account, you could assume that drinking unsweetened black tea or coffee before exercise could help you lose an extra 2 kilograms a year.

Practical tips for drinking tea and coffee for weight loss

If you really love your tea and coffee, and can't bear the thought of giving it up, then all is not lost. The research clearly suggests that if you want tea or coffee to help you lose weight, then you need to consume it black, and before you exercise. But remember that caffeine by itself does not help you burn more fat. It needs to be combined with exercise.

And if you want to minimise the weight-gaining effect, here's the lowdown on how to drink your cup of tea and coffee.

In the drink
• Try to gradually cut back on the amount of sugar you have in your tea or coffee. Your tastebuds will need around 4 to 6 weeks to adjust. If you can reduce your sugar intake by 2 teaspoons a day, that's nearly

3 kilograms less sugar you'll consume each year, or 60,000 kilojoules.
- To help reduce the kilojoules in coffee or tea, going without milk is ideal. But if you do have milk with your tea or coffee, try to switch to skim milk. If you only have one cup a day, and you only have a tiny bit of full-cream milk with it, then this isn't so much of a concern. But if you have a table-spoon of full-cream milk in four cups of tea or coffee each day, that's close to an extra kilogram of pure fat consumed each year (832 grams). Just like with sugar, your tastebuds may take a month or two to adapt.
- If you have a cappuccino or latte, choose the skinny- or lower-fat milk options. The amount of milk you consume will vary according to whether your coffee cup is small, medium or large, but you could be consuming between one and two cups of milk. Every cup of full-cream milk has 9.5 grams of fat and 300 kilojoules above and beyond what you'd get in a cup of skim milk.
- If you must have full-cream milk, go for the small-sized serving. And try not to make it an everyday drink.

With the drink
- Cut back on biscuits, pastries and cakes. Ideally, try to avoid eating anything with your tea and coffee.
- If you normally have two biscuits, cut back to one. If you only have one, only eat biscuits on the days you exercise. Try not to make biscuits an everyday food. Biscuits are full of fat, sugar, salt and kilojoules, and are low in anything resembling nature or good nutrition. They can be high in trans fats — the worst kind for your heart — while some popular biscuits contain more sugar than flour.
- Don't be fooled by packaging that claim the biscuits inside are 'low-fat'. Some reduced-fat biscuits are still frighteningly high in fat, and they may contain extra sugar, which means they can have a similar (high) kilojoule content to regular biscuits. It also highlights how bad the normal varieties are. If your goal is to lose weight, then walk right past the biscuit aisle of your local supermarket.

Associated behaviour
- Try not to use tea and coffee as a form of stress relief. Try to find other ways to help manage your stress.

- Avoid having tea and coffee within a few hours of going to bed — to minimise its impact on your sleep, both quality and quantity.
- If you drink tea and coffee, be aware that it can have a negative effect on your hormone balance, especially the fat-storing hormone insulin. Work on other strategies to keep insulin in check, such as regular exercise and a low-glycaemic-index (GI) diet.
- Don't just drink tea and coffee out of habit. If you have more than two cups of coffee or three cups of tea a day, your health will benefit by cutting back. Gradually reduce your intake, and really savour and enjoy the cups you do have.

CHANGES TO HELP YOU WITH YOUR WEIGHT LOSS	KILOJOULES SAVED	POTENTIAL WEIGHT LOSS OVER A YEAR
Buy 2 less lattes a week	650 over a week	Nearly 1 kilogram
1 less chocolate biscuit per day with your tea and coffee	2800 over a week	4 kilograms

How can it save you money?

You can save a lot of money by having less tea or coffee, by making it yourself, and by eating less junk food with it. Even a small change, like one less biscuit a day, can make a difference over time. Other small changes, like having less sugar or milk in your tea and coffee, will also amount to small savings. I have calculated the cost of a latte at $3, and the cost of a chocolate biscuit at $0.30. There is room to make your own calculations if the price you normally pay, or the quantity you consume, is different.

MONEY SAVED EACH WEEK	POTENTIAL TOTAL YEARLY SAVING
Buy 2 less lattes a week = $6 (approx.)	$312
1 less chocolate biscuit per day with your tea and coffee = $2.10 (approx.)	$109.20

SNACK SMART, SNACK LESS

How will it affect your weight?

Snacking can result in both weight loss or weight gain depending on some important variables. These variables are:

• **The quality of the snack**

Do you grab an apple or a chocolate bar when you're hungry? Is the snack healthy or high in kilojoules? High-kilojoule snacks such as potato chips, biscuits and chocolate bars are not going to help you lose weight. However, healthy snacks that are moderate to low in kilojoules can be a good weight-loss strategy, keeping hunger at bay until your next meal. Let's look at the kilojoule difference between some healthy, and not so healthy snack choices.

HEALTHY SNACK CHOICES	KILOJOULE CONTENT	LESS HEALTHY SNACK CHOICES	KILOJOULE CONTENT
Air-popped popcorn	1 cup — 130 kilojoules	Potato chips	50 grams — 1045 kilojoules
Raisin toast and 1 teaspoon jam	1 slice + jam — 380 kilojoules	Chocolate biscuits	2 biscuits — 830 kilojoules
Fruit salad	1 cup — 350 kilojoules	Sweet baked muffin	1 muffin — 1170 kilojoules
Banana smoothie (skim milk)	375 ml — 550 kilojoules	Soft drink	1 x 375ml can — 650 kilojoules

As you can see, healthy snack choices can more than halve your kilojoule intake or save you at least 300 kilojoules a day. And when you consider that snacks make up close to 30 per cent of some people's kilojoule intake this can make a big difference over time.

• **The portion size of the snack**

Even if you choose a healthy snack, you still need to watch how much of it you have. You can still eat too much of a good thing and take in too many excess kilojoules.

• **The portion size of your other meals**

Adding extra kilojoules in the form of snacks (healthy or otherwise) will work against you if the portion sizes of your main meals are still large. Remember, one of the secrets to losing weight is to reduce your kilojoule intake, not increase it. Snacking may help to prevent cravings and boost your energy levels. But snacking will only work for weight loss if you reduce the portion sizes of your main meals.

• **Your activity levels**

One of the keys to losing weight is to adjust your kilojoule intake to match your activity levels. You could call this the 'adjust as you go' strategy. You need to snack less and reduce your kilojoule intake on the days you don't exercise. In addition, it's important to not go overboard and eat too much on the days when you are active. Exercise can trigger a hunger sensation that is greater than your actual kilojoule needs, so drink plenty of water and eat slowly when you do eat.

Science says: Snacking doesn't actually promote weight loss

According to an Australian survey, more than half of the adult population tends to eat two to four times a day, while about 37 per cent eat more frequently (up to seven times a day). We like to snack. A study reported in the *Journal of the American Dietetic Association* found that the more often a person eats in a day, the more kilojoules they are likely to consume.

Another study, reported in *Psychological Bulletin*, found that another problem is the sheer variety of high-kilojoule snacks. The researchers claimed that when faced with multiple snacking options, people may eat beyond the point of hunger in order to get a taste of all that is before them. Put practically, a person who has a kitchen full of various goodies might chow down on more kilojoules than a person who has only one snack choice in their pantry.

This puts forward a good argument to cut back on snacks. It may be best for some people to keep their diets simple, and avoid snacking, or just limit themselves to one snack a day.

In addition, don't feel compelled to snack because you think it will help you lose weight. A recent study has put to rest the theory that snacking increases your metabolic rate. A team of researchers from the University of Newcastle had two groups of people eat the same foods and the same amount of kilojoules. However, one group divided their kilojoule intake into five or six portions, while the other group ate three square meals. The research found there was no significant difference in the amount of weight either group lost. It was previously thought that eating more often forced your body to spend more time digesting food, making it burn more kilojoules. But it now seems that frequent snacking as a weight-loss method is just a myth, and that the most important thing is how many total kilojoules we consume.

Still, there is one hidden messages to come out of this research. While snacking didn't increase weight loss, it didn't slow it down either, and so if you can keep your kilojoule intake under control, it's okay to snack if that's your personal preference. For some people, snacking between meals can prevent that ravenous hunger that potentially makes you overeat at the next main meal.

MYTHBUSTERS

Aren't low-fat snacks okay?

If you're talking about fruit and vegetables — yes. But a number of processed low-fat or reduced-fat foods, like biscuits, cakes, muffins, yoghurts, and ice-cream, still have significant amounts of sugar and kilojoules. Just because something is 97 per cent fat-free won't make the weight fall off you. Reduced-fat foods can also be very high in fat, even if they are lower than the regular variety. The reduced-fat content is usually replaced with sugar, so while you might eat a bit less fat, there is very little difference in kilojoules consumed. Research has shown that there is also a tendency for people to consume larger portions of fat-reduced foods or consume additional full-fat foods afterwards. People who received a yoghurt labeled as 'low-fat' consumed more kilojoules during their next meal than people with a nutritionally identical yoghurt labeled as 'high-fat'. So don't be fooled by the labels or eat more because it's low-fat. And don't go thinking that you can lose weight eating low-fat muffins or biscuits. Be aware that low-fat alternatives are only a better choice when you keep your portion sizes under control.

Practical tips to help change the way you snack

The following information includes general advice on snacking, and healthy snack ideas.

- Clear your home of any unhealthy snacks and stock up with healthy choices. If unhealthy snacks are harder to come by, you won't be so tempted to have them.
- Plan ahead by taking a snack with you to work, school or the park. That way you won't be tempted to have less healthy options. You can also take your own healthy snack foods to parties and social gatherings so there is at least one healthy choice available.
- Snack on exercise instead. Just as you might look towards a small snack to give you an energy boost or improve your mood, why not use exercise to do the same? One study found that chocolate lovers had reduced cravings after taking a brisk 15-minute walk. Short bites of activity can distract you when you're tempted to indulge and will also help keep hunger pangs at bay.
- Popcorn makes for a great snack but only if it's air-popped. Use spices such as cumin, cayenne pepper, garlic salt or chicken salt to add flavour without oil or butter. Oil-popped or movie theatre popcorn usually contains over three times the kilojoule content over air-popped.
- Fresh fruit, canned fruit and fruit salad are all a good snack choice, but they are all reasonably high in sugar, so don't go overboard. Fruits are often grouped with vegetables, like the advice to eat 'seven servings of fruits and vegetables a day'. This is misleading. Aim for four to six servings of water-rich vegetables (such as cucumbers, lettuce, zucchini), and limit your fruit intake to around two servings a day if your goal is fat loss.
- Nuts are a good snack but watch your portion size. Try to keep to a small handful, using nuts that haven't been roasted or salted such as cashews, almonds or walnuts. Buy them in bulk, and use small zip-lock bags to take with you.
- Try to vary the type of foods you snack on, which will make your food more enjoyable, and will help you get a wider range of nutrients from your diet. Ideally, snacks should be no more than 400 to 600 kilojoules. Here is a list of some healthy snack food ideas:
    - low-fat muesli bars
    - pretzels
    - canned tuna (in brine) with tomato on multigrain cracker bread
    - vegetable-based soups
    - vegetable sticks (carrot, celery, red capsicum) with salsa

- breakfast cereal and skim milk
- baked beans on toast
- rice cakes with ham, tomato, cottage cheese and pepper
- coloured Japanese rice crackers
- multigrain English muffins with marmalade
- wholemeal crumpets and creamed honey
- raisin toast with jam
- tomato salsa and vegetable sticks
- lite cup-a-soups
- low-fat cottage cheese and pineapple on toast
- low-fat custard and canned fruit
- low-fat yoghurt
- sorbet
- breakfast drinks (or other pre-made smoothies)
- flavoured bread sticks
- small portions of dried fruits with nuts and seeds
- flavoured rice cake discs

CHANGES TO HELP YOU WITH YOUR WEIGHT LOSS	KILOJOULES SAVED	POTENTIAL WEIGHT LOSS OVER A YEAR
Snacking a little less, or take your own healthy snacks with you	300 per day	3 kilograms

How can it save you money?

Having healthy snacks on hand, instead of buying snack foods when you are out and about, can certainly save you money. You can also save money by snacking less. The calculations are based on avoiding paying for three $3 snacks a week and supplying your own snacks at half the cost.

MONEY SAVED EACH WEEK	POTENTIAL YEARLY SAVING
Snacking a little less, or taking your own healthy snacks with you = $4.50 (approx.)	$234

PLAN YOUR MEALS IN ADVANCE

How will it affect your weight?

Managing your food intake when you are trying to lose weight is vital, but it's hard to pay constant attention to what and how much food is eaten. Planning your meals in advance is a great tool to help improve your diet and lose weight. Weight loss is just like any other aspect of your life in that the more planning and preparation you do, the more likely you are to succeed. Without a good meal plan, you are left to hunt and gather food in the modern world, making it hard to find healthy food choices if you aren't prepared.

Being organised helps you to avoid a last-minute crisis, and makes it much easier to stick to a healthy eating plan. In fact, meal planning can reduce some of the stress associated with cooking, and make meal times more enjoyable. Having healthy foods close at hand for breakfast, lunch, dinner and snacks will reduce the chances of grabbing junk on the run. It can also be helpful to know that you have planned ahead for a meal to extend for a lunch or another dinner, which can reduce the temptation to nibble on leftovers.

You don't have to be obsessive; but planning, organisation and structure can produce great results. If meal planning sounds a bit too organised or over the top, take a closer look at your breakfasts, lunches, dinners and snacks over the next few weeks. You'll probably see the same meals and recipes cropping up time and time again. Dinners often vary the most, but even then you'll probably have a few consistent favourites. Meal planning just increases the chances that your food choices will be healthy ones. And that can only help with weight loss. Have a look at the sample 7-day food plan at the end of this chapter.

Science says: I have a plan

A recent study reported in the *Japanese Journal of Nutrition and Dietetics* found that meal planning can make a difference to your level of body fat. Subjects who planned their meals reduced their portion sizes, while their weight, percentage of body fat and blood quality all significantly improved. Their dietary knowledge, attitude and behaviour were also said to have improved. Other studies have shown that making strategies such as meal planning part of daily life becomes easier and requires less attention over time.

And another study showed that chaotic households contribute to a mother's obesity. Household pressure was found to increase the possibility that a mother would be overweight. I've estimated that being better organised with your food and planning your meals in advance could help to reduce your kilojoule intake by 2 per cent a year. That kilojoule reduction is based on the fact that meal planning can help you eat healthier meals, reduce your portion sizes and reduce impulse purchases of junk food.

Practical tips for planning your meals

Preparation is a forgotten friend when it comes to weight loss. A few minor changes in your food preparation habits can make a big difference to your health and weight. Use these tips to help plan your meals effectively.

- Put aside 10 to 15 minutes each week at a set time on a set day to plan your next week's meals. Roughly plan out each breakfast, lunch, dinner and snack. Then put aside a minute or two at the end of each day to plan out the next day's food intake as you progress through the week.
- Plan your weekly meals by taking into account what's already in your fridge, pantry and freezer (and in your herb and vegetable garden, if you have one). Be mindful of using your perishables to save on waste.
- Write down your meal plan on paper or in a computer spreadsheet with a view to keeping them and reusing them to save time in the future. After you have 3 to 5 weeks' worth of meal plans, you can use them repeatedly.
- Plan on cooking extra quantities so that some meals can be used the next day for lunch or frozen for use at a later date. Weekends are a good time for doing extra cooking so that you don't have to cook every night of the week. Knowing you've got something that's quick and easy to heat up in the microwave makes it a lot easier to drive past that drive-through fast-food outlet on the way home.
- Use your plan to make a shopping list. It's well known that you shouldn't go shopping when you're hungry, but it can be just as

dangerous to go shopping without a list. The choices you make as you walk through the supermarket aisles will have a major impact on your body shape.

- Walk fast while you shop for groceries. You'll save time, burn more kilojoules and be less tempted to indulge in those treats that aren't on your shopping list.
- Work on building up your repertoire of healthy meals and snacks to use as the foundation of your meal plans. Use recipes that are low in kilojoules and low in animal fats.
- The best meal plans are those that are in sync with your weekly schedule and any events that arise in a given week. Factor in the nights when you are likely to get home late or have to race off to other activities.
- Involve the whole family in the decision-making process when deciding on your weekly menu. Giving kids a sense of ownership can also increase the likelihood that they will eat healthier meals.
- Keep things interesting by regularly experimenting with new foods and recipe ideas. You can mark out pages in recipe books or keep pages from magazines. You can then look through this stockpile of healthy recipes when you're planning out your meals each week.
- Don't feel defeated if you happen to stray from your plan. Sometimes, things just pop up that are unavoidable. It's important to remain flexible and aim for improvement, not perfection. After a blow-out, the key is get back onto your meal plan as soon as possible to minimise the damage.

CHANGES TO HELP YOU WITH YOUR WEIGHT LOSS	KILOJOULES SAVED	POTENTIAL WEIGHT LOSS OVER A YEAR
Planning your meals in advance	130 per day	1 kilogram

How can it save you money?

By being a little more conscientious with your shopping, cooking and storage of food, you could potentially save hundreds of dollars a year. That's because meal planning can help you to prevent food wastage. According to a 2005 study by the Australia Institute, adult Australians waste about 20 per cent of the food they buy. Put another way, one in every five grocery bags you purchase goes straight into the garbage. That's just like throwing money away. It's also been labelled as an environmental and financial disaster. There were a number of reasons given to explain food wastage, including that people cook or prepare too much, they don't use food before its use-by date, takeaways and leftovers don't get eaten, and drinks go unfinished. The major food items that are thrown away are fresh fruit and vegetables, although bread, meat, fish, dairy products, rice and pasta were also listed as common wasted items. I've based my calculations on the fact that meal planning can help prevent food wastage by 5 per cent, encouraging you to buy only what you need. When you consider that research shows food wastage can be up to 20 per cent of your grocery bill, then any strategy to help reduce that expense seems like a good investment of your time.

MONEY SAVED EACH WEEK	POTENTIAL TOTAL YEARLY SAVING
Planning your meals in advance = $8.70 (approx.)	$452.40

SAMPLE MEAL PLAN

	BREAKFAST	LUNCH	DINNER	SNACKS
MONDAY	wholegrain English muffin and grilled vegetables	minestrone soup	salmon and steamed Asian greens	1 mandarin low-fat natural yoghurt with sunflower seeds
TUESDAY	French toast with some fresh fruit	tuna and white bean salad	chicken and cashew stir-fry	1 apple hot chocolate made with skim milk
WEDNESDAY	porridge with sultanas and sunflower seeds	grilled steak and vegetable sandwich	grilled snapper and salad	1 orange small handful of mixed nuts
THURSDAY	chocolate banana smoothie	zucchini frittata	beef and bean casserole	tomato salsa and wholegrain cracker bread with cottage cheese 1 pear
FRIDAY	cereal, skim milk and fruit	ham and vegetable omelette	lamb and chickpea curry	handful of grapes 1 slice of raisin toast
SATURDAY	wholemeal pancakes with blueberries	hummus and tuna on pita bread	chicken and wholemeal pasta	low-fat yoghurt and walnuts 1 peach
SUNDAY	hot breakfast (poached egg, baked beans and grilled tomato on multigrain toast)	baked sweet potato with tuna and tomato salsa	lemon chicken with fried rice	strawberry smoothie 3–5 dried apricots

This 7-day menu plan is an edited extract from the 21-day menu plan from *The H-Factor Diet* (ABC Books, 2009).

REDUCE OR REMOVE BUTTER AND MARGARINE ON YOUR BREAD

How will it affect your weight?

Cutting down on the amount of fatty spreads you put on bread and toast is a sure-fire way to accelerate your weight loss. Both are extremely high in kilojoules and should really be minimised or even eliminated if your goal is reduce body fat. By having one less tablespoon of butter or full-fat margarine each day, you will consume a massive 5.5 kilograms less fat each year. That's one small change that really stacks up over time.

Science says: Less dietary fat equals less body fat

Fat is the most energy-dense nutrient, with twice the kilojoule content per serving compared to carbohydrates and protein. According to a recent report in the journal *Obesity*, cutting back on dietary fat is the most efficient way to stop the obesity epidemic. They reported that diets with fewer fats can reduce your energy intake by 400 kilojoules a day, which is thought to be enough to stop the growing epidemic of overweight and obesity. Eating less fat, particularly less saturated and trans fat, can easily help to reduce your energy intake. They also discussed the fact that very low-fat diets are hard to sustain; however, moderate-fat diets can be maintained over time. This was demonstrated in a study which found that a low-fat diet (33.3 grams a day versus 51.3 grams a day) and higher in fibre, fruit, and vegetables produced greater weight loss over 5 years. They discussed the fact that a healthy option for those who want to lose weight is easily achieved by cutting out small amounts of fat from each meal. Cutting back on the amount of butter or margarine you put on bread is exactly the type of behaviour that can help you lose weight.

Isn't margarine better than butter?

The question of which is the better spread depends on what perspective you are asking from. From a weight-loss perspective, there are some better and worse choices (and there are well over fifty to choose from). In general, butter contains 4 grams of fat per teaspoon (about what you'd put on sandwich) and 152 kilojoules. Full-fat margarines have a similar kilojoule content to butter, however, the light spread varieties contain 2 grams of fat and 73 kilojoules per teaspoon. That's half the kilojoule content, which would make a big difference over time. From a heart health perspective, you need to look at the risks associated with the different types of fat in butter and margarine. Yes, butter is more 'natural', but more than half of its fat content is saturated. That's the type of fat that increases the bad (LDL) cholesterol and ups the risk of heart disease. Margarines are made with vegetable oil and their fats are chemically altered to make it solid, and spreadable, just like butter. Chemically altered trans fats are even worse for your heart than saturated fats because they not only increase the bad (LDL) cholesterol, they also lower the good (HDL) cholesterol. But Australian margarines (except for cooking margarines) are a lot lower in trans fats than they used to be. In fact, they should really be called spreads, because they are not manufactured in the same way as margarine any more (containing less fat and more water). Check the labels and see for yourself. The best choice for your heart includes spreads that are low in both trans fat and saturated fats. Some basic spreads and canola spreads have no trans fats at all, and are still low in saturated fats. These margarine spreads are much higher in 'good' fats (polyunsaturated and monounsaturated) compared to butter. There are also some butter-based products that are combined with liquid vegetable oils to reduce their saturated fat content. So, for your heart, the new light spreads seem okay, with dairy blends next best in line followed by the highly saturated and artery-clogging butter. In saying that, the best choice for your heart is a little olive oil, avocado and hummus on your bread instead of either butter or margarine. And finally, from a taste perspective, it really comes down to your personal choice. Whatever your taste, enjoy butter or margarine in small quantities.

Practical tips to cut out butter and margarine

Here are some suggestions on how you can cut back on your butter and margarine intake.

- One simple way to halve your intake of butter or margarine on sandwiches is to spread it only on one slice of bread.
- Take it a step further and cut out fatty spreads altogether.
- When having a salad sandwich, use avocado, hummus, low-fat cream cheese, spreadable cottage cheese, low-fat mayonnaise, chutney, relish and pickles.
- To prevent Vegemite from being a bit dry, have it with low-fat cottage cheese on toast or sandwiches.
- Substitute with light cream cheese, which has a quarter of the fat content of butter. Just make sure you spread it just as thinly as you would butter.

CHANGES TO HELP YOU WITH YOUR WEIGHT LOSS	KILOJOULES SAVED	POTENTIAL WEIGHT LOSS OVER A YEAR
Eating one tablespoon less of butter or margarine a day. (That's what you'd put on about four slices of bread.)	610 a day	5.8 kilograms

How can it save you money?

Simple really — the less you use, the less it costs you. Now I know butter and margarine are not that expensive, but this is one of those little changes that really adds up over time. For the calculations, I have used the average price of $2.50 for a 500 gram tub.

MONEY SAVED EACH WEEK	POTENTIAL TOTAL YEARLY SAVING
Eating one tablespoon less of butter a day = $0.56 (approx.)	$28.75

REDUCE THE SIZE OF YOUR MEALS

How will it affect your weight?

Portion size is vital for weight control because the bigger your serving, the bigger your kilojoule intake. If you don't burn off all the kilojoules you eat, no matter how healthy they are, you will gain weight, or find it difficult to lose weight. We also know that a number of things have changed in the last 20 to 30 years that makes it easier to consume larger portions. This includes larger chocolate bars, potato chip packets, soft drink cans, plate sizes, fast-food restaurant portion sizes, glasses of wine and even cookbook serving sizes. Overcoming portion distortion can go a long way towards helping you reduce your kilojoule intake, and your body-fat levels. In fact, this is one of the easiest ways to modify your diet. You don't have to change what you eat at all, just eat a little less of it. We know the average Australian consumes 6500 kilojoules a day. Reducing your portion size by just 5 per cent could help to reduce your kilojoule intake by approximately 325 kilojoules a day.

Science says: Portion size is a major barrier to weight loss

Studies show that most people eat more than the recommended serving sizes for many foods. It is estimated that today, we consume 600 additional kilojoules daily beyond the average from just twenty years ago. People also tend to eat what's put in front of them. One study showed that when two groups had access to unlimited lasagna, the group who first received a large portion ate more than the group who were first given a small portion, even though both groups were allowed to get up for more. Finally, reducing your portions can also have an impact on the size and capacity of your stomach. A study conducted at the Obesity Research Center in New York demonstrated that obese subjects had a stomach capacity up to 40 per cent more than lean subjects.

Doesn't water dilute your digestive juices
if you combine it with food?

There's no scientific evidence to support the belief that water dilutes digestive juices or stomach acid, or interferes with proper digestion. One of the few scientific studies to address this issue, reported in the *American Journal of Clinical Nutrition*, found that water ingestion did not alter glycaemic and insulin response. In fact, digestive juices work best in a semi-fluid environment. This myth may have started because people with digestive ailments like acid reflux or hiatus hernia may experience a worsening of symptoms if they drink water with their meals. But for the majority of people without digestive ailments, your body is more than capable of handling some water with every meal. Drinking more water with meals can help reduce portion size.

Practical tips for reducing your portion size

Portion size is one of the most underestimated factors in our rising obesity epidemic. Sometimes it's not just what food you're eating, but how much of it you have. Take on board the following tips for eating at home and also while you're out, to help reduce your portion sizes.

- Be wary of your portion sizes of high-kilojoule foods, such as biscuits, cakes, pastries, desserts, fats, oils, spreads and high-GI carbohydrates.
- Don't eat in front of the television as the distraction can cause you to overeat.
- Use a smaller plate when serving yourself food, and smaller glasses when serving yourself kilojoule-laden drinks.
- Store leftovers in individual portions rather than in bulk containers.
- Adjust your serving sizes according to your activity levels. In other words, eat a little less on the days you don't exercise.
- Use a food diary to get a more comprehensive picture of the quantity of food you are eating.

- While it might seem tedious to weigh your food, even doing it just once can make you more aware of what a normal serving size is. This may be a worthwhile exercise if you are struggling with portion sizes.
- Don't reduce your portion sizes of water-rich vegetables.
- Eat slowly and savour your food. It takes 10 to 20 minutes for your brain to get signals from your stomach that you are full. By eating slowly, you will eat less.
- Wait a few minutes before getting a second helping. Your fullness from your first helping will be more likely to register, and the craving may pass.
- Sometimes hunger is actually a signal from your body that you are partially dehydrated. Drinking plenty of water can help take the edge off hunger and cravings by keeping your stomach full between meals.
- Eat plenty of fibre and lean protein. These two nutrients have the best potential to make you feel full for the least amount of kilojoules.
- Eat more natural foods. Unprocessed foods such as beans, peas, lentils, fruit and vegetables are absorbed slowly, making you feel fuller for longer. When it takes longer for your hunger to return, cravings are reduced, and you tend to eat smaller portions.
- Eat less, more often. Overeating and consuming large meals can stretch your stomach wall, meaning you need to eat more to feel full. Have smaller meals more often to help minimise the capacity of your stomach.
- If you're eating out at a restaurant, share an entree or dessert instead of having it all to yourself.
- Don't feel obliged to eat everything that's put in front of you. Don't let others determine your portion size. If you're at a restaurant and you've had enough, ask for a doggie bag.

CHANGES TO HELP YOU WITH YOUR WEIGHT LOSS	KILOJOULES SAVED	POTENTIAL WEIGHT LOSS OVER A YEAR
Reducing your portion sizes by 5 per cent	325 a week	3 kilograms

How can it save you money?

If you cut down your portion sizes and total food consumption by approximately 5 per cent, then you can cut your food bills by 5 per cent. Remember, the average person spends $174 a week on food and drink. If that figure doesn't match your weekly spend, there's room to make your own calculations.

MONEY SAVED EACH WEEK	POTENTIAL TOTAL YEARLY SAVING
Reducing your portion size by 5 per cent = $8.70 (approx.)	$452.40

EAT SLOWLY

How will it affect your weight?

It's not just what you eat that can have an impact on your weight, but how fast you eat it. Eating too quickly can actually cause you to eat too much, and make it harder to lose weight. If you are busy or distracted during a meal, you are more likely to overeat. The stomach has stretch sensors that send 'stop eating' signals to your brain after you have eaten enough. But it takes time for the brain to register fullness, with estimates that this can take 10 to 20 minutes. In other words, if you eat fast, you can continue to eat even when your stomach has had enough. It takes about 1 hour of exercise to burn off what you can eat in 5 to 10 minutes. By taking this simple but powerful step of slowing down the speed that you eat, you will need less food to feel full. It takes a few extra minutes to finish each meal, but it can make a dramatic difference to your weight, and your health. There are also nutritional advantages from eating slower, because when you chew your food more thoroughly, you will absorb more nutrients from it. Chewing physically breaks down food, and the smaller a food particle is when it reaches your digestive tract, the more nutrients you will absorb. This can also help to prevent digestive problems.

Science says: Slow eating is both slimming and satisfying

Eating slowly with smaller mouthfuls has been proven to help people to eat less, and reduce their kilojoule intake. A study reported in the *American Journal of Clinical Nutrition* found that people who took smaller mouthfuls and had more time ate 281 kilojoules less than subjects who ate the same meal with a larger spoon as fast as they could. The subjects were instructed to eat a meal of pasta and sauce with a small spoon in small bites, to chew each mouthful thoroughly, and to rest between mouthfuls. The fast eaters took in an average of 2713 kilojoules in 9 minutes, while the slow eaters consumed 2432 kilojoules, or 10 per cent less, in 29 minutes. The researchers theorised that eating at a slower speed allows more time for the body's natural fullness signals to kick in, and people can have their hunger satisfied with fewer kilojoules. Eating a hurried meal was thought to actually cause overeating because stomach distension and appetite-related hormones take time to tell the body that it's time to stop eating. The other fascinating thing about this study was that the slow eaters reported feeling fuller and more satisfied both immediately after as well as 1 hour after their meal. They also rated their meal as more pleasant. In other words, slower eating will not only reduce your kilojoule intake, but it can also add to the enjoyment of eating. This really is significant, because if you are going to stick to a healthy eating plan over time, you need to enjoy it. A different study found that when people ate lunch while sitting at a table that has been set, they consumed a third less at a later snack than those who ate their midday meals while standing at a counter. The researchers suspected that if you treat every dining experience with greater respect, you'll be less likely to use your fork as a shovel. Standing up while eating could create a sense of urgency, while sitting down at a set table creates a sense of formality, and that may boost fullness levels.

Practical tips for slowing down your eating speed

It might seem simple enough, but the speed at which you eat is a habit, and slowing it down may take a bit of work. Following are some strategies you can use to eat a little slower.

- Savour your food and take time to enjoy the taste, aroma and texture of each mouthful. Take small bites and chew your food thoroughly.
- Have a small pause, take in a few breaths, or enjoy a small sip of water between mouthfuls.
- Use small eating utensils and serving dishes.
- If you are going to eat a treat, such as chocolate or ice-cream, slow is the go. Really enjoy the taste and texture of the food, and keep your portions small. It's important not to deprive yourself of any food — avoid the mentality of dieting.
- Taste your food and enjoy it. Be in the moment, and mindful of eating a little slower. Slowing down may also help to make you more aware of your hunger. This is sometimes referred to as 'mindful' eating. Start to think about how hungry you are before you eat, and how your hunger is removed as you eat.

• Try to avoid using external cues to tell you when to stop eating, such as when your plate is clean, when everyone else at the table is finished, or when a TV show is over. Try to rely on internal signals by only eating when you're hungry, and only having enough to no longer feel hungry (rather than to feel full). Eat until you are satisfied, but not feeling that you can't fit anything else in. This may take a conscious effort for a while, but it can help to gain control over food.

CHANGES TO HELP YOU WITH YOUR WEIGHT LOSS	KILOJOULES SAVED	POTENTIAL WEIGHT LOSS OVER A YEAR
Eating slowly for one meal every day	216 a day	2 kilograms

How can it save you money?

We know that eating slower reduces your kilojoule intake by 10 per cent, and it could do the same for your food bill (saving over $900 a year). However, it might be a bit too much to expect you to eat slower for every meal, every day. So I've used 3.33 per cent in my calculations, based on the fact that it seems reasonable that you could slow down your eating speed for at least one meal a day. If you feel like you could eat more than one meal a day slower, or alternatively that once every day is too much, there's room to make your own calculations.

MONEY SAVED EACH WEEK	POTENTIAL TOTAL YEARLY SAVING
Eating slowly for one meal every day = $5.80 (approx.)	$300

MAKE YOUR OWN HEALTHY LUNCH

How will it affect your weight?

While it might seem easy to duck down to the local café at lunchtime and grab a quick bite, it can be hard to find healthy options. Making your own lunch instead of buying it will almost always result in a better choice for weight loss. It gives you control over your midday meal, and makes it less likely that you will fall back on quick-fix, high-kilojoule choices when you are hungry and rushed. Not only will a healthy lunch help to control weight, but it can also boost your concentration and energy levels, and prevent you from feeling sluggish throughout the afternoon. Try to include some quality carbs and a lean protein source with some nutrient-rich vegetables to keep your body and mind energised. These foods also help to stabilise your blood sugar levels, reducing hunger later in the day. As with all meals, try to keep your portion size moderate, otherwise you might end up feeling like you need an afternoon siesta.

Science says: Ditch the takeaway lunch

A recent AC Neilsen poll (2006) found that almost two-thirds (61 per cent) of Australians eat takeaways for lunch during the week, with hot chips (24 per cent), hamburgers (19 per cent) and meat pies (19 per cent) on the menu. And one in five Australians ate their lunch while at their desk or on the move. As you can see from these statistics, a lot of Australians would benefit from changing their lunch habits. I've estimated that making your own healthy lunch could reduce your kilojoule intake by 200 kilojoules a day. However, it could be a lot more, depending on how much you usually rely on takeaways.

Practical tips for making your own lunch

The following tips will help to make sure the lunch you prepare is enjoyable while still low in kilojoules and high in essential nutrients.

- Try to make your lunchtime carbohydrates with the least amount of processing. Use low-glycaemic carbohydrates, such as multigrain sliced bread, wholemeal bread rolls, grainy cracker breads or brown pita bread. Use high-fibre white bread if you don't like multigrain breads.
- Include a lean protein source. Lean meats such as canned fish, roast beef, chicken breast or low-fat ham are ideal. These are preferable to salami, pastrami, corned beef or devon. Other protein alternatives include peanut butter, hummus and ricotta cheese, but use sparingly, as these are higher in fat.
- Sneak in some vegetables by adding lettuce, sprouts, cucumber, tomato or roasted vegetables such as capsicum, eggplant, mushroom, zucchini or Spanish onion into your sandwiches.
- Keep your sandwiches tasty and interesting by regularly changing the type of bread, protein and vegetable foods.
- Vegetable-based soups are a tasty and healthy alternative to sandwiches. If you don't have the facilities to heat it up at work, use a thermos.
- When you are cooking, make double the portion and store the leftovers in a food container for the next day. Foods that are ideal include stir-fries, curries and casseroles.
- Cook up a big meal that freezes well every few weeks so you always have a steady supply of soups or vegetable pasta sauces. Freeze them in lunch-sized portions. Knowing you have a healthy, tasty lunch available for a quick re-heat can reduce your reliance on the less healthy options.
- If you struggle to have enough time in your morning, make your lunch the night before. You can always make your lunch for the next day while you are making dinner.
- If you are going to take sandwiches to work, purchase a good quality lunchbox with divided panels and room for a small frozen drink or ice brick. You can always place tomato in some clingwrap or in a small container and put it on your sandwich just before eating if you are worried about the bread going soggy. If the food is fresh, you will be more likely to enjoy it.
- In the warmer months, why not take a salad to work. Include lots of greens, tomatoes, asparagus, and cucumber, include some protein in the form of lean meats and combine with some healthy fats in the form of avocado or nuts and seeds. Keep your dressing light in fat, but high in

flavour by combining just a little olive oil with flavoured vinegars or citrus juice.

• Wraps are a healthy and convenient lunch option that gives you a break from a traditional sandwich. Just include some lettuce, lean meat, tomato, grated carrot and mustard.

• Vegetable dips make a great lunch. Have some salsa, hummus or baba ganoush with some cracker bread or vegetables sticks (carrot, celery, capsicum).

• If you are at work, take a genuine break and get away from your desk. Get out of the office and take the time to enjoy your meal. You've gone to the trouble of making it, take the time to enjoy it.

CHANGES TO HELP YOU WITH YOUR WEIGHT LOSS	KILOJOULES SAVED	POTENTIAL WEIGHT LOSS OVER A YEAR
Making your lunch 1 day a week	200 a week	¼ of a kilogram
Making your lunch 5 days a week	1000 a week	More than a kilogram

How can it save you money?

This is a fairly popular money-saving tip, and it can save you a lot of cash if you work and regularly buy your lunch. It's a great example of how small changes can make a big difference over time. Yes, it will take a little extra time out of your day, but once you get into a routine of making your own lunch, it really shouldn't be too much trouble at all. For the calculations, I've estimated it would cost $1.50 to make your own ham and salad sandwich, while it would cost $6.50 to buy one at a café or sandwich bar (average of three prices in different suburbs). If these prices vary from what you pay to make your own lunch, there is space to make your own calculations.

MONEY SAVED EACH DAY	POTENTIAL TOTAL YEARLY SAVING
Making your lunch 1 day a week = $5 (approx.)	$240 (48 working weeks)
Making your lunch 5 days a week =$25 (approx.)	$1200 (48 working weeks)

DRINK WATER INSTEAD OF SOFT DRINK OR FRUIT JUICE

How will it affect your weight?

The type of beverage that you choose will have a dramatic effect on your body shape, especially if you look at the effect over time. For example, swapping a daily can of soft drink for an extra glass of water will save you around eleven teaspoons of sugar per can, which also works out at around 14 kilograms of sugar a year. And to burn off that amount of sugar each year, you'd have to walk over 1000 kilometres, which is roughly the same distance as walking from Sydney to Melbourne. Amazing when you look at what a small change can do over time. Any kilojoules you drink will make it harder for you to lose body fat because they provide virtually no fullness for an equivalent kilojoule amount of a solid food. In fact, the kilojoules you drink virtually make no difference when it comes to satisfying your hunger. Liquid kilojoules in the form of soft drinks, fruit juice, sports drinks, energy drinks, flavoured mineral water and cordial are all very similar from a fat-loss perspective. The easily digested sugars from these drinks gives you extra kilojoules that must be utilised before your body will burn off stored body fat. A glass of fruit juice has a similar kilojoule content to a glass of regular soft drink.

Science says: Drinking water decreases obesity

A study reported in the *Journal of Pediatrics* revealed that encouraging kids to drink water instead of juice and soft drinks reduced their risk of being overweight by an amazing 31 per cent. The study examined over 3000 children in schools where water fountains were installed, kids were given refillable water bottles and taught the benefits of drinking water. By drinking an additional 200ml of water each day, the incidence of obesity was reduced dramatically. Another study, reported in the *Journal of the American Dietetic Association*, showed that drinking 500 millilitres of water 30 minutes before a meal can help to reduce the kilojoule intake of that meal. The study was based on the fact that as soon as the volume of food in your stomach reaches a certain size, the receptors in your stomach send the 'full' signal to your brain. As shown in the table, the group that had a pre-meal drink of water ate 13 per cent less kilojoules at that meal compared to people who had a drink.

SIZE OF DRINK BEFORE MEAL	KILOJOULES CONSUMED AT MEAL
No water	2410 kilojoules
500ml	2100 kilojoules

MYTHBUSTERS

Isn't fruit juice healthier than soft drink?

Fruit juice is promoted as a healthy drink, and is even mentioned as a replacement for whole fruit. But this is not necessarily the case. Fruit juice actually has a very similar kilojoule content to a glass of regular soft drink. It may contain a few extra trace minerals and a fraction more fibre, but from a fat-loss perspective, there is very little difference. You need between three and four oranges to make one cup of juice, so you get all the kilojoules but lose the fibre and some of the nutrients. In other words, you will still feel hungry after eating the equivalent of three oranges. Drink water instead, and eat fruit whole as nature intended.

Practical tips for drinking more water

Your body loses around 2 litres of water every day through sweat, your breath, and when you go to the toilet. It's important that you replace that lost fluid for your body to function at its best. Kilojoule-free water is the best choice for your weight and health, and here are some helpful tips to up your intake.

• Drink one to two glasses of water before breakfast, lunch and dinner. The extra fullness may also help to reduce your portion sizes.

- Don't wait to feel thirsty. Try to make drinking water a habit by adding it on to other habits, such as after going to the toilet or after brushing your teeth.
- Drink a little extra water if it's hot, if you are active, or if you work in an air-conditioned office. Consume 150 to 200 millilitres of water for every 15 to 20 minutes of exercise.
- Have a water bottle at your desk, in your fridge and in your car.
- Be more aware of your water intake as you get older. Between the age of 60 to 70, people start to lose their appetite, and get less water from foods in their diet.
- If you take medications that have a diuretic effect, or if you use fibre tablets, include an extra glass of water each day.
- Drink water to quench your thirst, and only drink other kilojoule-laden beverages in small amounts for taste.
- If you don't like water straight up, add a lemon, lime or orange slice.
- Don't keep juice, soft drink or cordial in your house. If it's hard to get, you'll be less likely to have it.
- If you must have fruit juice, have less, or watering it down to reduce the kilojoule content.
- Vegetable juices have a much lower kilojoule content than fruit juice, because they don't contain the same concentrated sugars (except beetroot).
- Give your tastebuds time to adjust to drinking less sugar-laden drinks. Just like cutting sugar out of your tea or coffee, it takes a while to adjust, but you will get used to it.

CHANGES TO HELP YOU WITH YOUR WEIGHT LOSS	KILOJOULES SAVED	POTENTIAL WEIGHT LOSS OVER A YEAR
1 less 250ml glass of fruit juice per day	440 a day	4 kilograms
1 less can (370ml) of soft drink per day	650 a day	6 kilograms

How can it save you money?

Water out of a tap is the ideal alternative to soft drink and fruit juice. It's virtually free, and is 100 per cent kilojoule free. You can save thousands of kilojoules and hundreds of dollars every year by making this one small change.

In addition, if you can drink a little more water, you can further reduce your kilojoule intake (and your food spend) because water can help make your stomach feel fuller and reduce your appetite. If you are out at a restaurant, water is usually free, and a much cheaper alternative to juice or soft drink. I have averaged out the price for a glass of fruit juice and soft drink at 50 cents. If you mainly drink juice at home after buying in bulk, then you won't be paying that much. But if you get your juice from a petrol station, vending machine or juice bar, you'll be paying much more. And one final reminder — water out of a tap is more than 1000 times cheaper than bottled water.

MONEY SAVED EACH WEEK	POTENTIAL TOTAL YEARLY SAVING
1 less 250ml glass of fruit juice per day = $3.50 (approx.)	$182
1 less can (370ml) of soft drink per day = $3.50 (approx.)	$182

EAT IN, COOK MORE AND EAT OUT LESS

How will it affect your weight?

We know that the more often you eat out, the more likely you are to be overweight. We also know that people are relying on convenient foods more than ever before. In the 1980s, approximately $1 in every $20 was spent on food consumed outside the home. Now, according to the Better Health Channel, it's $1 in every $3. That's a third of our food bill spent on takeaways, fast food and restaurant meals. Dependence on fast food can become an automatic behaviour with negative consequences. When people work long hours, it's common to feel too tired to prepare healthy meals. Suddenly, choosing high-fat fast food becomes the norm. Junk food has even been described as addictive. Our modern society has been labeled as 'obesogenic' — an environment flooded with high-kilojoule junk food that makes it easy to gain weight, and hard to lose it. If there is always food around you, it's hard not to eat more. This can be seen in the popularity of shops selling cakes, cookies and coffee, along with super-size meal deals and the fast food culture. It's no wonder nearly two-thirds of adults are overweight. Whenever you eat away from home, you subject yourself to this obesogenic society. By cooking more at home, you can regain control over your diet, and your kilojoule intake.

Science says: Cook yourself thin

Research has shown that meals prepared outside the home can contain up to 50 per cent more kilojoules, with more fat and larger portion sizes. They also contain less fibre. Some fast foods can deliver your recommended daily kilojoule and fat intake in one meal. The perception that eating out is a 'special occasion' may also encourage you eat more than normal. I've estimated by eating one less takeaway meal per week, you could consume at least 1000 kilojoules less by cooking a meal instead. A recent study conducted at the Cardiovascular Research and Education Foundation found that home-cooked foods made from fresh ingredients had less sugar, salt, fat and starch. Subjects who ate at home had a higher percentage of 'good cholesterol', lower blood pressure and were more insulin sensitive than those who ate out four or more times per week. If you are insulin sensitive, your body releases less of the fat-storing hormone insulin. And another study found that only 3 per cent of kids' meals served at fast-food restaurants met basic nutritional guidelines. The argument is pretty strong that eating junk food is dangerous for your health and your waistline.

MYTHBUSTERS

Isn't the occasional treat okay?

I think it's very important to indulge occasionally. Depriving yourself just doesn't work because you end up wanting it even more. Feelings of deprivation, denial, bingeing and guilt are not part of the solution to healthy eating or long-term diet change. But there also needs to be a balance. What does the words 'occasional treat' really mean? How often is 'occasional', and how big is your portion size of the 'treat'? How many other 'treats' have you had that week? With such a wide variety of junk food out there, people might have pizza once a week, but they also have fried chicken once a week, and hamburgers once a week, then takeaways another night. If you are serious about fat loss, try to aim for 5 to 6 days a week when you stick to a healthy eating plan. Don't have treats every day.

Practical tips for cooking more and eating out less

The global financial crisis has seen the sale of junk foods skyrocket. Sadly, people don't want to cook, don't know how to cook, or don't understand that healthy eating doesn't have to cost more. The reality is that cooking more for yourself can help you lose weight, can help you save money, and can also be extremely rewarding. Here are some general tips on how to cook more at home, and eat less junk food.

- Improve your cooking skills. By developing your own skills in the kitchen, you can learn how to make healthy foods taste great, prepare meals in advance, and get adventurous with all those wonderful budget superfoods (see page 132). Get a hold of some healthy recipe books, or sign up for a cooking class.

- Get your kitchen into shape. Your kitchen is an environment within your control, so it's important to surround yourself with equipment that makes healthy cooking easier and more enjoyable. Some helpful equipment to have includes a good set of non-stick pans and utensils, good quality storage containers, a good knife, a steamer and a food processor.
- If you aren't sure what you'd like for your birthday or at Christmas, ask for some kitchen gadgets to help inspire. Ideas include an indoor grill, a salad spinner, a marinating brush, a citrus zester, a well-stocked spice rack or a recipe file organiser.
- Create your own healthy versions of fast-food favourites at home, such as pizza, hamburgers, and Thai food. Being able to limit the amount of cheese, oil and fat used to prepare these foods can still leave room for plenty of flavour, but cut back on all the kilojoules. Go to the end of this section for three healthy fast-food recipes.
- If you are going to eat food prepared outside your home, try to make the healthiest choices available.
- Eating out can still be enjoyable without destroying your attempts at weight loss. The following ideas can help to minimise the damage.

AT RESTAURANTS

- Stop when you're full, and don't feel like you have to clean your plate.
- Learn to make special requests, such as having sauces served on the side.
- Become a regular customer of restaurants with the healthiest menu.
- Drink plenty of water instead of alcohol, fruit juice or soft drink. This can also help to make you feel full.
- If you must have desserts and entrees, share them, and don't have both.
- Look for foods that are baked, steamed, roasted or grilled.
- Choose lean meats with lots of salad or vegetables.
- Order an entree size for your main meal, and ask for a side order of steamed or roasted vegetables.
- Avoid battered foods, pastry, creamy sauces or foods fried in oil or fat.

FOR TAKEAWAYS

- Some of the healthier choices available include tomato-based sauces with pasta, thin crust pizza with vegetable or seafood toppings, sushi, grilled fish and salad (hold the chips), plain hamburgers (leave out the cheese or bacon), skinless chicken and kebabs with minimal meat and creamy sauces (go for lots of salad, and sweet chilli sauce).
- Don't supersize your meals. Avoid extra chips and soft drinks.
- Avoid anything battered (chicken nuggets), deep-fried (chicken) or covered in a cream sauce (ready-made pasta). A good alternative is barbecue chicken (remove the skin) with vegetables such as corn cobs, peas and baked potatoes.
- For Asian foods, avoid fried rice, fatty meats like duck, or battered dishes (dim sims). Instead, go for steamed rice, steamed dim dims and dishes with lean meats and lots of vegetables.
- Try to make foods such as hot dogs, pies, sausage rolls, spring rolls, and hot chips a very occasional food (less than once a month).

CHANGES TO HELP YOU WITH YOUR WEIGHT LOSS	KILOJOULES SAVED	POTENTIAL WEIGHT LOSS OVER A YEAR
Eating 1 less takeaway meal per week	1000 a week	1.5 kilograms

How can it save you money?

Eating out has been identified as one of the top causes of personal debt. Remember that a third of our grocery bills is spent on food prepared outside the home, so the more you cut back on eating out, the greater your potential to save. After you cut back on takeaway food, and replace it with healthy food cooked at home, you should have a little extra money left over. I'll estimate that you'll be about $7 ahead each week.

MONEY SAVED EACH WEEK	POTENTIAL TOTAL YEARLY SAVING
Eating 1 less take away meal per week = $7 (approx.)	$364

Healthy fast food recipes

VEGETABLE PIZZA

Serves 2 to 4

1 wholemeal pizza base
1 tablespoon tomato paste
1 tablespoon barbecue sauce
1 tablespoon finely chopped garlic
½ small Spanish onion, finely chopped
½ cup finely chopped mushrooms
½ cup drained pineapple pieces (optional)

½ red capsicum, finely sliced
1 zucchini, finely sliced
¼ cup grated low-fat cheese
spray of oil
2 teaspoons finely chopped mixed fresh herbs, such as basil, parsley or thyme

Preheat the oven to 220°C.

Mix together the tomato paste, barbecue sauce and garlic and spread over the pizza base.

Stir-fry the vegetables for 2–4 minutes in a non-stick pan until the vegetables are tender. Drain off any liquid.

Sprinkle the vegetables and cheese evenly over the pizza base.

Lightly spray a non-stick pizza or baking tray. Place the pizza base on the prepared tray and bake for 10–20 minutes or until the cheese is golden.

Sprinkle herbs over the top just before serving.

Hint: Add other vegetables, such as roasted pumpkin, corn kernels or asparagus spears. You could also dollop on some hummus or baba ganoush for extra flavour.

HAWAIIAN BEEF BURGER

Serves 2

150g extra-lean minced beef
½ small onion, finely chopped
½ cup fresh wholegrain breadcrumbs
1 egg, lightly beaten
salt and pepper to taste
2 wholegrain rolls (suitable for hamburger buns), split in half

small handful of lettuce leaves
2 slices pineapple, drained
1 small tomato, sliced
2 tablespoons barbecue sauce

Place the beef, onion, breadcrumbs, egg, salt and pepper into a bowl and mix together well. Divide the beef mixture into two even portions and shape into patties. Place a non-stick pan over a medium heat and cook the patties for 4–5 minutes each side or until cooked. Drain on paper towels. Toast or grill the halved buns until golden. Top a half of a bun with a cooked patty, lettuce, 1 slice pineapple, slices of tomato, and 1 tablespoon of barbecue sauce. Place the other half of the bun on the top and serve immediately.

Hint: Make double the meat mixture, form into patties and freeze the uncooked portions.

CHICKEN PAD THAI

Serves 4

½ teaspoon oil (sesame has lots of flavour, though any oil will do)	1 teaspoon fish sauce (optional)
	1 teaspoon lime juice
1 teaspoon crushed garlic	1 cup shredded cooked chicken
1 tablespoon finely grated ginger	1 cup (100g) cooked flat noodles
1 carrot, cut into strips	½ cup bean sprouts
½ cup broccoli florets	1 bunch coriander, finely chopped
½ finely chopped red capsicum	½ teaspoon chilli powder or
1 tablespoon crunchy peanut butter	1 fresh chilli, finely chopped
1 tablespoon Hoisin sauce	(optional)
1 tablespoon soy sauce	

Heat the oil in a non-stick pan on high heat. Add the garlic, ginger, carrot, broccoli and capsicum, and stir-fry for around 2 minutes. Add a little water if required.

Add the peanut butter, the sauces, lime juice, chicken and noodles, and heat through.

To serve, sprinkle with sprouts, coriander and chilli.

PART 4

THE BIG SEVEN: BUDGET SUPER-FOODS AND RECIPES

The next tips of *The Tight Arse Diet* focus on my seven budget superfoods. These are tasty, low-cost foods available in your supermarket that can help you lose weight, and save money. You'll find more information on each of the foods, with tips on how you can prepare them to maximise your weight loss. I've also included a number of healthy recipes using the budget superfoods. And while these recipes are lower in kilojoules, I hope you'll discover they are also high on flavour and taste. Try to eat them every day or as often as you can to maximise your weight loss, and your savings.

1. EAT MORE EGGS

How will it affect your weight?

Eggs are almost the ideal weight-loss food. Their high protein content helps to fill you up, reduce sugar cravings, and makes it easier to stick to a reduced kilojoule eating plan. One egg contains around 6.5 grams of protein, and only has around 300 kilojoules. Practically speaking, eating an egg or two for breakfast can help you to resist snacking later in the day. Nutritionally, they are almost like a multivitamin, containing a wide range of nutrients such as iron, and vitamins A, B, E and D. Eggs are also high in iodine, which is essential for healthy thyroid function, which produces the hormones that keep your metabolic rate firing.

Science says: Proven weight-loss benefits from eggs

A study published in the *International Journal of Obesity* showed that eating two eggs for breakfast, as part of a low-kilojoule diet, helped overweight adults lose 65 per cent more weight and feel more energetic compared to people who ate a bagel breakfast of an equal kilojoule value. Subjects who ate eggs felt fuller after breakfast and stayed fuller for longer than those who ate a bagel. Although the kilojoule content of both meals was the same, the egg group ate 2400 kilojoules at lunch, compared with the average 3050 kilojoules eaten by the bagel group. That's a massive 29 per cent fewer kilojoules. Even if the difference was only 10 per cent, this could have a massive impact on your body shape over time. The egg-eaters also ate fewer total kilojoules over the day. This is further supported by another study, conducted at the Rochester Center for Obesity Research, which found that eating eggs for breakfast helps limit your kilojoules intake all day by more than 1600 kilojoules. Because of their high protein content, eggs have a much greater capacity to fill you up than breakfast cereal or bread.

Aren't eggs bad for your cholesterol levels?

People were once reluctant to eat eggs due to their high cholesterol content. However, we now know that there is a difference between dietary cholesterol (in eggs) and blood cholesterol. As it turns out, it's actually saturated fat in your diet that is more likely to raise blood cholesterol levels rather than eating foods rich in dietary cholesterol. One egg yolk contains around 5 grams of fat, with only 1.5 grams of saturated fat, and the rest as healthy fats. Egg whites contain no fat. Compare that with a cup of reduced-fat milk, which contains 3 grams of saturated fat. People who are trying to lose weight are often encouraged to only eat the egg whites because they provide quality protein with zero fat. I must confess to giving this advice myself in the past, which was current at the time. But the yolks are full of nutrients and additional quality protein, and the recommendations about them have changed. Remember, we were once advised to put butter on burns, vinegar on bluebottle stings, and eat the least amount of fat as possible in your diet — all advice which can actually make matters worse instead of better. Well, sometimes new research gives us new knowledge and new understanding. Despite the health recommendations of the past, it's seems okay to have at least an egg each day, and in moderation, they will not increase your blood cholesterol levels. For example, the researchers in the eggs versus bagels study in the 'Science says' section found that the levels of HDL and LDL cholesterol, as well as triglycerides, did not change in the daily egg-breakfast-eaters over the 2-month study. A daily egg, or seven eggs a week, should pose no threat if you are in good health, you know your blood cholesterol levels are healthy, and you limit other sources of animal fats. But before going to town on eggs, it is important to factor in your personal circumstances, such as your current heart health and health history (if you are genetically predisposed to high cholesterol). It's also important to look at the rest of your diet. For example, it's often the foods eaten with the eggs that can be a problem. Foods such as buttered toast, bacon, sausages, hash browns and hollandaise sauce are all high in saturated fat, and could have a negative impact on your cholesterol levels. If you have any of the risk factors for heart disease, such as a family history, high blood pressure or cholesterol, diabetes, excess weight or you smoke, you may wish to discuss your egg intake with your doctor.

Practical tips for including more eggs in your diet

To make sure the way you eat and prepare eggs helps with your weight loss, rather than holding it back, follow these tips.

- Eggs are a versatile and easy-to-prepare breakfast choice; however, for weight control, the best low-kilojoule choices are boiled or poached eggs, or scrambled eggs made with skim milk and minimal oil, butter or cream. It's also best to have your egg without bread or butter.
- Be wary of the company that eggs keep at breakfast. You can still enjoy a hearty warm breakfast of eggs accompanied by grilled low-fat ham, grilled mushrooms, grilled tomatoes, baked beans, steamed spinach and steamed asparagus.
- Make pancakes with one egg, one cup of skim milk and one cup of wholemeal flour.
- Eggs don't just have to be for breakfast. Hard-boiled eggs can be used in salads or, as a snack, on cracker bread with tomato and cracked black pepper. You can also mash a hard-boiled egg with canned fish, low-fat ricotta and grated carrot for a tasty sandwich filling.
- Have an omelette or vegetable frittata for lunch.
- Make healthy fried rice by mixing cooked, chopped vegetables, ham and a chopped boiled egg with cooked rice. Stir-fry in sesame oil, add a splash of soy sauce and cook until heated through.
- Mix together beaten egg with pesto or tomato salsa and a little reduced-fat cheese, cracked black pepper and fresh herbs. Stir through just-cooked wholemeal pasta for a quick and easy dinner or lunch. Serve with a green salad.
- Fortified eggs, rich in omega-3 fatty acids, may cost a little more, but are a good source of this important nutrient, especially for people who don't like eating fish or other seafood.

CHANGES TO HELP YOU WITH YOUR WEIGHT LOSS	KILOJOULES SAVED	POTENTIAL WEIGHT LOSS OVER A YEAR
Eating 2 eggs for breakfast 3 times a week instead of a low-fibre choice (bagel, white bread toast, low-fibre breakfast cereal)	650 a day or 1950 a week	3 kilograms

How can it save you money?

At an average price of only $5 per dozen (or 42 cents each), eggs are one of the most affordable high-quality protein foods in the marketplace. There aren't many better budget superfoods. They're also convenient and last for several weeks in the fridge, meaning there is rarely any waste. The price can vary depending if the eggs are free range, barn laid, organic or fortified.

By eating eggs for breakfast, studies have shown you will eat 29 per cent fewer kilojoules in total for the rest of the day, and potentially save on your food bills. I have used a more conservative figure of 10 per cent for the calculations, which are also based on the fact that the average person spends close to $25 a day on food. For the annual savings figure, I have assumed that you would have eggs for breakfast three times a week. If this doesn't match your dietary circumstances, there is room to make your own calculations.

MONEY SAVED EACH WEEK	POTENTIAL TOTAL YEARLY SAVING
Eating 2 eggs for breakfast 3 times a week instead of a low-fibre choice (bagel, white bread toast, low-fibre breakfast cereal) = $7.50 (approx.)	$390

Healthy egg recipes

TOMATO AND HERB OMELETTE

Serves 2

spray of oil
1 teaspoon crushed garlic
½ cup drained corn kernels
½ cup roughly chopped tomatoes
1 teaspoon finely chopped fresh basil
    or ½ teaspoon dried basil
3 eggs
⅓ cup skim milk

½ teaspoon ground paprika
salt and cracked black pepper,
    to taste
2 slices of wholegrain toast, to serve
1 teaspoon grated Parmesan cheese
1 teaspoon finely chopped fresh
    parsley or ½ teaspoon dried
    parsley

Lightly spray a non-stick frying pan with oil and place over a medium heat. Add the garlic, corn, tomatoes and basil to the frying pan and cook for 2 minutes. Remove from the frying pan and set aside in a warm place.

Lightly respray the pan. Beat together the eggs, milk, paprika, salt and pepper. Pour into the pan, swirl the mixture to cover the base of the pan and cook until the mixture sets.

Add the tomato and basil mixture to one half of the omelette, then slip a spatula under the other half of the omelette and fold over. Divide the omelette in half and serve each half on a slice of wholegrain toast, with the Parmesan and parsley sprinkled on top.

Hint: You can also add or substitute other vegetables, such as mushrooms, baby spinach, cooked asparagus, finely sliced capsicum or grated carrot.

COOKED BREAKFAST

Serves 1

1 egg
2 slices low-fat ham
½ tomato, grilled
⅓ cup baked beans

1 slice multigrain toast
    (no butter)
salt and cracked black pepper,
    to taste

Bring a saucepan of water to a gentle boil. Gently lower in the egg and boil to your taste (see the hint below). Cool slightly.

Place a non-stick pan over medium heat. Add the ham, tomato and baked beans and stir occasionally until warmed through.

To serve, pour the bean mixture over the multigrain toast. Peel and slice the egg and arrange on the plate. Season with salt and cracked black pepper.

Hint: Bring the egg to room temperature before using. When the water is boiling gently, carefully place the egg on a spoon and lower it into the water. Start timing from when the water re-boils. Timing depends on the size and degree of hardness desired. Generally it's 3–4½ minutes for soft-boiled, 4½–6 minutes for medium-boiled and 6–7 minutes for hard-boiled.

VEGETABLE FRITTATA

Serves 2

1 cup finely chopped vegetables
    (eg broccoli, capsicum, corn, green
    beans, pumpkin, zucchini, spinach)
¼ cup finely chopped green onions
4 eggs

2 tablespoons grated Parmesan
    cheese
salt and cracked black pepper,
    to taste

Heat a lightly sprayed non-stick frying pan over a medium heat. Add the vegetables and green onions and cook for 2 minutes or until the vegetables are slightly softened. Leave in the frying pan.

Whisk together the eggs, Parmesan cheese, salt and cracked black pepper and pour over the vegetables.

Reduce the heat to low, and cook until the frittata is set around the edge but still runny in the centre.

Cover the frying pan with a lid or baking tray and continue cooking the frittata for 3–5 minutes or until set. (Alternatively, place under a grill set at medium heat to finish cooking.)

Hint: Serve warm with a side salad and tomato relish. You can also let the frittata cool and pack it for a picnic lunch.

2. PREPARE YOUR OWN POTATOES

How will it affect your weight?

Potatoes are a versatile budget superfood. Rich in fibre and minerals, they are a comfort food that can fill you up. But their influence on your weight can be both positive and negative depending on how they are prepared. Firstly, the healthiest part of the potato is the skin or peel (good news if you hate peeling spuds). You lose a lot of the potassium and vitamin C by removing the skin, and 60 per cent of the fullness-giving fibre; keep the peeler in the drawer. This make smaller potatoes a better choice, because smaller the potato, the higher the proportion of skin to starch. Next, let's look at their glycaemic index, or GI. Potatoes, like all carbohydrates, are digested into glucose, which is absorbed into the bloodstream to supply fuel or energy. However, not all carbohydrates release glucose into the bloodstream at the same rate. The GI ranks foods on how quickly they release glucose into your bloodstream. The faster a food increases your blood sugar levels, the higher the insulin response will be to reduce the escalating blood glucose levels. Insulin triggers your body to store glucose and, importantly, fat. Foods that release glucose slowly (low-GI foods) trigger little if any insulin release, which helps to minimise fat storage. Low-GI foods are known to be more filling, delay hunger pangs for longer, and/or reduce energy intake for the remainder of the day compared with their high-GI counterparts. Potatoes are generally classified as a high-GI food, which is not ideal if you want to lose body fat. However, there are ways you can serve potatoes that help to reduce the GI. A cold potato salad made with vinaigrette dressing, stored overnight in the fridge, is by far the healthiest way to eat potatoes. The cold storage increases the resistant starch content of potatoes by more than a third (see 'Science says') and the acid in the vinaigrette (whether you make it with lemon juice, lime juice or vinegar) will slow stomach emptying. This also reduces the need for the fat-storing hormone insulin. One study, reported in the *European Journal of Clinical Nutrition*, found that these changes to the humble spud (boiled, cold-stored and served with a vinaigrette) reduced the potatoes' GI by 43 per cent. Finally, let's look at significant difference that cooking methods can make to the humble potato. Traditionally, potatoes were a staple of the meat and three vegetables diet. Now, potatoes are eaten less with meals, and more as fatty snack foods like chips. Potatoes have virtually no fat, but processed potato foods have a lot of fat added to them.

POTATOES	KILOJOULES PER 100 GRAMS
Baked	275
Mashed (with milk)	310
97 per cent fat-free potato wedges, home-baked	546
Roast potato, in oil	630
Potato wedges, commercial	750
Potato chips, straight cut, commercial	1030
French fries	1155
Potato chips	2100

As you can see, the smaller and thinner the potato gets, the greater the surface area for the fat to be absorbed, and the greater the kilojoule content. For example, potato chips have nearly ten times the kilojoule content of a baked potato. What you have to accompany your potato can also make a big difference. A healthy baked potato becomes another thing entirely when smothered in sour cream, gravy or butter. An important weight-loss strategy with potatoes is to prepare them yourself with minimal additional fat.

Science says: Potato salad please!

Most fibres and starches are digested and absorbed into your body through the small intestine. Resistant starch is a unique type of fibre found in cooked, cooled potatoes that your body finds hard to digest. This type of starch is also found in other carbohydrate foods such as cooked, cooled pasta and rice (think pasta salad and sushi), legumes, and unique breads, pastas and breakfast cereals made with added Hi-Maize (made from a special breed of corn). Resistant starch is created when starchy foods are 'cooled'. When a potato is cooked, it absorbs water and swells, but when it cools, much of the starch crystallises forming 'resistant starch'. Because these foods 'resist' digestion, it arrives in larger pieces in your intestine. Once there, bacteria ferment it, producing fatty acids that are absorbed into your bloodstream. These unique fatty acids actually help with weight loss by changing the way the body burns fat as fuel. They are thought to block the body's ability to burn carbohydrates and encourage fat-burning sooner. Usually carbohydrates are used first for fuel, but when resistant starch is present, stored body fat and recently consumed dietary fat is used earlier as an energy source. Researchers reported in the *Journal of Nutrition and Metabolism* that replacing just 5.4 per cent of carbohydrates with resistant starch increased fat-burning (the use of fat as fuel instead of carbohydrates) by 23 per cent. Resistant starch in a meal is associated with less fat storage after that meal and, over the long term, that could help to significantly reduce the storage of body fat. An additional study, reported in the *Journal of the American College of Nutrition*, showed that when normal flour is replaced with a flour alternative that is high in resistant starch, the kilojoule content of that food is reduced. This is another way that resistant starch can contribute to weight management and weight loss.

MYTHBUSTERS

Shouldn't I cut out all fat?

While dietary fat is high in kilojoules and the most likely food to be stored in your fat cells, don't cut it out completely. Focus on plant and seafood fats that supply energy and essential nutrients to fuel your day. This includes moderate portions of avocado, fish and seafood, linseed oil, olive oil, nuts and seeds in your diet. Avoid animal or processed trans fats, such as butter, margarine, pastries and junk foods. These fats take longer to digest and have been linked with an increased risk of developing cardiovascular disease.

Practical tips for eating more potatoes

Potatoes are a budget-food phenomenon. Here are some tips on how to make sure they are a weight-loss phenomenon as well.

- The small, washed chat or new potatoes are the best choice of potato, but only if they are unpeeled.
- The healthiest way to cook potatoes is microwaved, boiled, steamed or baked (although baking does reduce the vitamin and mineral content).
- The best way to eat potatoes is in a cool potato salad with a vinaigrette dressing. If you want to add mayonnaise, try to use a low-fat variety or replace half the mayonnaise with low-fat natural yoghurt.
- If you like baked potatoes, the good news is that Australian food scientists are working on developing a lower-GI variety. But until then, use an oil spray or minimal fat, keep your portion sizes small and keep the skin on.
- If you like mashed potatoes, replace half the potato with mashed cannellini beans (white beans) to reduce the GI. Use herbs, garlic, spices, mustard, skim milk and minimal oil to add flavour to your mashed potatoes instead of full-cream milk or butter.
- For a variation of baked potatoes in their jackets, bake or boil a few small chat potatoes, and top with kidney beans, salsa, cottage cheese and fresh herbs for a tasty lunch or dinner.
- Add potato chunks, skin on, to soups, stews and casseroles.
- Make a change from ordinary spuds and substitute lower-GI root vegetables, such as sweet potato, carrots or beetroot.
- Lower the GI of potatoes by serving them with other vegetables in a side dish. Halve some baby potatoes and place in a baking tray with some sliced Spanish onion, strips of red capsicum and zucchini. Toss with some peeled garlic cloves, olive oil and red wine vinegar. Bake for 30–40 minutes at 180°C.

CHANGES TO HELP YOU WITH YOUR WEIGHT LOSS	KILOJOULES SAVED	POTENTIAL WEIGHT LOSS OVER A YEAR
Having a baked potato instead of frozen fries or wedges once a week	755 a week	1 kilogram
Having a baked potato instead of potato chips once a week	1825 a week	2.5 kilograms

How can it save you money?

Potatoes are incredibly cheap, especially if you prepare them yourself. The following calculations are based on the savings you could make from baking your own potatoes (0.25c per 100 grams) versus buying frozen chips once a week (0.35c per 100 grams) and potato chips ($2.20 per 100 grams).

MONEY SAVED EACH WEEK	POTENTIAL TOTAL YEARLY SAVING
Having a baked potato instead of frozen chips once a week = 10 cents (approx.)	$5.20
Having a baked potato instead of potato chips once a week = $1.95	$101.40

Healthy potato recipes

POTATO SALAD WITH GRAIN MUSTARD VINAIGRETTE

Serves 4

20 small, new potatoes, washed and halved
20 fresh green beans, topped and tailed
12 ripe cherry or grape tomatoes, halved
1 tablespoon olive oil
1 tablespoon white wine vinegar
1 tablespoon lemon juice
1 tablespoon grain mustard
2 tablespoons finely chopped fresh herbs, such as dill, parsley or mint
salt and cracked black pepper, to taste

Steam or boil the potatoes for 10–15 minutes until just cooked. Drain and refrigerate for 3–4 hours.

Boil or steam the green beans for about 5 minutes or until they turn bright green. Drain and rinse in cold water (to stop the cooking process).

Place the potatoes, green beans and tomatoes in a small bowl. Whisk together the remaining ingredients and pour over the vegetables. Toss gently to combine and serve as a side salad.

POTATO SKIN WEDGES

Serves 2 to 4

spray of olive oil
5 large potatoes, skin on, scrubbed
and cut into wedges
salt to taste

¼ cup low-fat natural yoghurt
(optional)
2 tablespoons sweet chilli sauce
(optional)

Preheat the oven to 200°C.

Cover a baking tray with aluminium foil and spray lightly with olive oil spray.

Place the potato wedges on the foil, and spray lightly with olive oil spray. Sprinkle with salt and bake for 40–45 minutes, turning occasionally, until the potatoes are crisp.

Serve the cooked wedges hot, with low-fat natural yoghurt and/or sweet chilli sauce as dipping sauces.

Hint: Sprinkle with additional herbs and spices, such as chilli powder, lemon pepper, Cajun spices or rosemary, if desired.

MEXICAN POTATOES

Serves 1

3 very small potatoes (skin on),
washed and halved
1 tablespoon canned red kidney beans
(or baked beans)

1 tablespoon canned creamed corn
1 tablespoon tomato salsa
1 teaspoon sweet chilli sauce
1 tablespoon low-fat cottage cheese

Place the potatoes in a microwavable dish. Cover and cook on High (100 per cent) for 4–6 minutes or until tender.

Place the beans, corn, salsa and sweet chilli sauce in a small microwavable container and cook on High for 1 minute or until heated through.

Spoon the bean mixture over the potatoes and dollop the cottage cheese on top.

Hint: You can also add fresh herbs, green onions, hot sauce, a little avocado or low-fat cheese.

3. EAT MORE OATS

How will it affect your weight?

Eaten as muesli in summer or porridge in winter, oats have gone from prison food to power food. Oats are a good source of protein, vitamins, minerals and healthy fats. They are also a low-GI carbohydrate, so they release glucose slowly, helping to minimise the release of insulin, the body's fat-storing hormone. From a fat-loss perspective, oats have one of the highest levels of soluble fibre of all grain foods. The soluble fibre forms a gel in your digestive tract capturing fluids and delays the emptying of your stomach. This helps to satisfy your hunger and can also help to prevent you from feeling hungry for quite some time. In other words, oats give you longer lasting energy for less kilojoules. Oats with water and skim milk is a very satisfying, low-kilojoule option for breakfast.

Science says: Start with oats and become less hungry

A recent study conducted by the Rippe Lifestyle Institute looked at the weight-loss effect of eating oats for breakfast as part of an overall reduced-kilojoule weight-loss plan. It was found the subjects lost significant amounts of weight and body fat when compared to control subjects who didn't eat oats. Over the 12 weeks of the study, the oat-eating subjects (who also walked for 15 to 30 minutes a day) reduced their waist circumference by 5 centimetres and reduced their body fat level by 5 per cent. It was also highlighted that 80 per cent of the weight loss was from loss of fat, with lean muscle mass largely preserved. The researchers observed that oats are an ideal breakfast for people trying to lose weight because you will be less likely to feel hungry later in the morning. This has been confirmed by other studies, which have shown that oats maintain normal blood sugar levels longer than most other foods, helping to reduce hunger, and making a reduced-kilojoule eating plan more satisfying. Another way that oats can help keep hunger at bay was shown in additional research, where low-GI foods like oats were shown to stimulate a greater release of hormones in the stomach, creating a 'full' sensation. When comparing oats with other breakfast cereals, the kilojoule content is fairly similar per equivalent serving.

Aren't muesli bars healthy?

While oats themselves are a very healthy food, if you cover them with chocolate or yoghurt, you've got a whole different story. Some muesli bars are so high in kilojoules that'd you'd be better off eating a rich chocolate confectionery bar. Most muesli bars are held together with a sticky mix of various sugars, which doubles their sugar content, halving the fibre content. Some muesli bars are also high in saturated fat and should really sit alongside the chocolates in the supermarket aisle.

Practical tips for eating more oats

One of the tastiest, cheapest and healthiest ways to include more wholegrains in your diet is to eat oats. Here are some tips on how to do that.

- Make porridge with skim milk and water, and sweeten with berries, sultanas, banana, peaches, low-fat yoghurt or a minimal amount of sugar or honey.
- Make your own natural muesli by adding different nuts and seeds, and a small amount of shredded coconut or dried fruits (see the recipe below).
- Avoid the commercial crunchy (toasted) mueslis that are baked in fat, as well as the pre-flavoured varieties that are high in sugar.
- Add oats to soups, casseroles, smoothies and home-made biscuits or muffins.

How can it save you money?

Oats are a dream come true for people wanting to lose weight. They are tasty, versatile and can fill you up cheaply. If only they could help to pay off your mortgage as well! To determine how many kilojoules you can save, I have worked out that you may eat 5 per cent fewer kilojoules over the rest of the day because oats fill you up more than other low-fibre cereals. This could also potentially save you money. While I haven't calculated this in any cost savings in the table, we do know that oats are cheaper for an equivalent serving. The costing used in the calculations are based on average prices from three Australian supermarkets. The annual savings figure is based on having oats instead of another cereal on 3 days each week.

CHANGES TO HELP WITH YOUR WEIGHT LOSS	KILOJOULES SAVED	POTENTIAL WEIGHT LOSS OVER A YEAR
Eating 40 grams of oats versus 40 grams of cornflakes on 3 days each week	325 a week	1.5 kilograms
Eating 40 grams of oats versus 40 grams of corn, oats and wheat cereal on 3 days each week	325 a week	1.5 kilograms

MONEY SAVED EACH DAY	POTENTIAL TOTAL YEARLY SAVING
Eating 40 grams of oats versus 40 grams of cornflakes on 3 days each week = 15 cents (approx.) [25c for cornflakes, minus 10c for oats]	$23.40
Eating 40 grams of oats versus 40 grams of corn, oats and wheat cereal on 3 days each week = 27 cents (approx.) [42c for corn, oats and wheat cereal, minus 10c for oats]	$42.12

Healthy oat recipes

NATURAL BIRCHER MUESLI

Serves 2 to 4

½ cup rolled oats
½ cup skim milk
200ml low-fat yoghurt
½ Granny Smith apple, cored and grated (skin left on)

2 tablespoons sultanas
½ teaspoon ground cinnamon
2 tablespoons slivered almonds
1 tablespoon sunflower kernels

Combine the oats, milk, yoghurt, apple, sultanas and cinnamon in a large bowl. Cover and refrigerate overnight.

Sprinkle the almonds and seeds over the oat mixture just before eating. **Hint:** If you like your muesli thicker, use slightly less milk. If you like it thinner, add some extra skim milk or low-fat soy milk. You can also add a little honey if you like slightly more sweetness. This recipe is only limited by your imagination. You can add different types of nuts and seeds. You can also substitute virtually any fruit you like for the apple, such as chopped banana, strawberries, peaches, berries, dried apricots, plums, pears, passionfruit, dates or prunes. Or make up your own fruit combination.

OAT AND FRUIT PANCAKES

Serves 2 to 3

⅓ cup rolled or quick-cook oats
1 large egg, lightly beaten
low-fat cottage cheese
¼ teaspoon ground cinnamon
½ cup berries (any combination of strawberries, raspberries and blueberries)

low-fat yoghurt, low-fat ice-cream or maple syrup to serve ¼ cup (optional)

Place the oats in a blender or food processor and process for 1 minute. Remove and transfer to a small mixing bowl.

Add the egg, low-fat cottage cheese and cinnamon and mix together lightly.

Pour ladlefuls of the batter into a lightly sprayed non-stick frying pan. Cook over a medium-high heat. When the surface of the pancakes bubbles, turn the pancakes over. Repeat with the remaining mixture and respray the frying pan as required. Keep the pancakes in a dish in a warm oven until ready to serve.

Add the berries to a blender or food processor and process to make a purée. Pour over the pancakes and serve immediately. Add a little low-fat yoghurt, low-fat ice-cream or maple syrup, if desired.

MUESLI SLICE

Makes 12 pieces

1 cup rolled oats
½ cup white self-raising flour
½ cup wholemeal self-raising flour
½ cup brown sugar
¼ cup bran flakes
1 teaspoon ground cinnamon

1 egg, lightly beaten
½ cup sultanas
½ cup roughly chopped dried apple
1 cup skim milk
spray of oil

Preheat the oven to 180°C.

Combine all the ingredients except the oil and mix well.

Lightly spray a non-stick 20cm x 30cm oven tray (or a lamington tray). Place the mixture on the tray, roll out to an even thickness and press slightly. Smooth the top.

Bake for 40–50 minutes or until golden brown.

Cut into bars while still hot.

Hint: Use chopped dried apricots instead of the apple or sultanas if desired. You can also add ¼ cup of chopped walnuts, although this will add to the fat and kilojoule content of the slice.

4. EAT MORE PULSES

How will it affect your weight?

Another fantastic budget superfood that can help you lose weight is pulses (sometimes called legumes). This group of foods includes beans, chickpeas and lentils, either canned or dried and ready for soaking. Pulses are pretty much the ideal fat-loss food, giving you maximum fullness for minimum kilojoules. They are an excellent source of protein, low-glycaemic-index carbohydrates, essential nutrients and fibre. They are one of the best foods for regulating your blood sugar and insulin levels and making you feel full. They are also high in a unique type of fibre called resistant starch. See 'Prepare your own potatoes' on page 140 for more information on the weight-loss benefits of resistant starch.

Science says: Pulses are a filling and hormone-balancing food

Research has shown that consuming pulses may lessen the amount of insulin required to control blood sugar levels. This slow rise in blood sugar gives pulses the distinction of being a very low-GI food, which prevents the release of the fat-storing hormone insulin.

According to the journal *Appetite*, low-glycaemic-index (GI) foods delay the return of hunger, decrease subsequent food intake, and increase the sensation of fullness compared to high-glycaemic-index foods. The results of several studies suggests that low-glycaemic-index diets also result in significantly more weight or fat loss than high-glycaemic-load diets. As an added bonus, this makes pulses a great source of long-lasting energy for your body. Other studies have confirmed that the resistant starch in legumes can make changes to the way your body uses fuel. Resistant starch has been observed to help the body use as much as 25 per cent more fat as fuel for up to 24 hours after a meal that includes pulses. I have used this figure of 25 percent in the table to calculate the fat-reducing benefit of having legumes instead of meat twice a week. I have also used the national average of 91 grams of fat a day in my calculations

(Australian Bureau of Statistics). Note that the focus on this particular tip is on fat burning. You may not necessarily burn too many extra kilojoules, but you will use a higher proportion of fat as fuel compared to glucose. This can still make a significant difference to your body shape and your health.

MYTHBUSTERS

Don't beans make you fart?

This one is not a myth. Beans do make you fart. Pulses contain fibres and carbohydrates that are difficult to digest, forming lots of gas when they reach our intestines. When you combine that with their high protein content, you have a near perfect fart food. Yet gas is a perfectly natural and unavoidable by-product of digestion. If you weigh up all the benefits of pulses, it's a small price to pay. If you are concerned, try adding mustard seed to lentils and beans while cooking, which is thought to reduce the gas-producing effect of pulses.

Practical tips for eating more pulses

If the only legumes you've ever eaten are baked beans and a little hummus dip, it's time to step out of your comfort zone. Pulses are a great partner for many foods and dishes. Following are some ideas on how you could include more pulses in your diet.

- Look for ways to include pulses in your diet at least four to five times a week. One serving is roughly three heaped tablespoons of beans.
- Canned varieties of pulses such as chickpeas and beans save you the hassle of soaking overnight before cooking, and are just as good. Just rinse off the salty water before cooking with them. Lentils, black-eyed peas and split peas don't need to be soaked and are great in soups.
- Hummus is a versatile food. In a food processor, combine a tin of drained chickpeas with a dash of lemon juice, a pinch of ground cumin, garlic, salt, fresh herbs and a couple of tablespoons of low-fat natural yoghurt and blend until smooth for a tasty spread. You can also make the same dip using cannellini beans instead of chickpeas. Sprinkle with paprika for some added spice.

- Replace some of the meat in your recipes with beans, peas or lentils. Use red lentils in soups, pasta sauces, burgers, stews and curries or make your own dhal. Add lentils puréed or whole, depending on the texture you prefer.
- Use red kidney beans in a shepherd's pie or chilli con carne.
- Use refried beans in burritos.
- Add white cannellini beans or chickpeas to a green salad sprinkled with fresh mint leaves.
- Have a warm breakfast that includes baked beans.
- Add beans and chickpeas to salads for a protein hit.

How can it save you money?

Pulses are often described as the poor man's meat and are an inexpensive and nutrient-rich substitute for animal protein. By having pulses instead of meat twice a week (or substituting half the meat with pulses, as shown in the Mexican Shepherd's Pie recipe that follows), you can save money on your grocery bill. For the following calculations, I have calculated mince at $10 a kilo, and red kidney beans at $3.75. Those prices just take into account one recipe that includes mince. If you substitute beans for more expensive cuts of meat, your savings could be considerably more. There is room to make your own calculations if these prices or meal frequency rates don't match your circumstances.

CHANGES TO HELP YOU WITH YOUR WEIGHT LOSS	KILOJOULES SAVED	POTENTIAL WEIGHT LOSS OVER A YEAR
Having 200 grams of beans instead of 200 grams of meat twice a week	1710 a week	2 kilograms

MONEY SAVED	POTENTIAL TOTAL YEARLY SAVING
Having 200 grams of beans instead of 200 grams of meat twice a week = $2.50 per week (approx.)	$130

MEXICAN SHEPHERD'S PIE

Serves 4

250g lean minced beef

1 medium onion, finely chopped

2 cloves garlic, crushed

½–1 teaspoon chilli powder

2 teaspoons ground cumin

400g fresh or canned tomatoes,
   roughly chopped

300g can red kidney beans, drained

1 tablespoon flour

spray of oil

2 large potatoes (350g)

350g can cannellini (white) beans,
   drained

¼ cup skim milk

¼ cup dried breadcrumbs

1 tablespoon Parmesan cheese,
   grated

1 teaspoon paprika

Preheat the oven to 220°C.

Heat a non-stick pan over a high heat. Add the beef, onion, garlic, chilli powder and cumin. Cook until the beef is browned.

Add the tomatoes, beans and flour and stir until the mixture comes to the boil.

Lower the heat and simmer, uncovered, for about 10 minutes or until the mixture has thickened. Spray an ovenproof dish with olive oil and spoon in the mince mixture.

Boil, steam or microwave the potatoes until tender, then drain. Mash the potatoes with milk and stir until smooth.

Place the cannellini beans in a food processor and pulse until smooth. Stir the beans through the mashed potatoes.

Gently spread the potato and bean mixture over the meat mixture then sprinkle with breadcrumbs, Parmesan cheese and paprika. Bake for about 30 minutes or until the top of the pie is lightly browned.

CHILLI BEEF CASSEROLE

Serves 4

500g rump or round steak, fat
  removed, cut into bite-sized pieces
1 medium onion, finely chopped
¼ cup red wine
175g mushrooms, sliced
1 red capsicum, deseeded and sliced
½–1 teaspoon chilli powder (to taste)
1 tablespoon tomato paste

2 tablespoons plain flour
440g can tomatoes, roughly
  chopped
1 beef stock cube
300g can red kidney beans, drained
salt and cracked black pepper,
  to taste

Heat a large non-stick saucepan over high heat and dry-fry the beef and onion until the meat has browned on the outside. Remove the meat and onion and set aside in a warm place. Deglaze the saucepan with half of the red wine, add the mushrooms and cook for 3–4 minutes.

Add the chilli powder and tomato paste and cook for a further 2 minutes. Add a little water to the flour to make a smooth paste. Add to the pan and stir through.

Add the tomatoes and remaining red wine to the mixture and bring to the boil.

Return the beef to the pan. Add the crumbled stock cube and kidney beans. Season to taste with salt and cracked black pepper.

Simmer for 10 minutes and serve with steamed vegetables or a small serving of brown rice.

Hint: This recipe freezes well so make a double batch to have on hand for another meal.

HUMMUS

Makes 1½ cups

400g can chickpeas, drained
   and well rinsed
2 tablespoons lemon juice
2 tablespoons tahini (ground
   sesame seed paste)
2 tablespoons water
1 tablespoon olive oil

1 teaspoon ground cumin
1 teaspoon paprika
1 teaspoon crushed garlic
salt and cracked black pepper,
   to taste
fresh parsley or mint, finely
   chopped, to garnish

Place the chickpeas, lemon juice, tahini, water, olive oil, cumin, paprika, garlic and seasoning in a food processor and pulse until smooth. Add a little extra lemon juice or water until the hummus is the consistency you prefer.

Transfer to a serving bowl and sprinkle with the herbs.

Hint: This dip is perfect with pita bread, wholegrain crackers, raw vegetables or spread on sandwiches. You can also add roasted capsicums or sundried tomatoes for extra flavour.

5. EAT MORE SEAFOOD (CONDITIONS APPLY)

How will it affect your weight?

Not only is fish and seafood one of the best protein sources available, it also offers a number of health and fat-reducing benefits. The type of fat in seafood, called omega-3 fatty acid, can help with weight control in a number of ways, including:

* Lowering your blood triglyceride levels

Triglycerides are the type of fat that, in excess, is stored in the fat cells. Keeping these at a lower level makes it harder for your body to store fat.

* Improving glucose tolerance

People with impaired glucose tolerance have higher than normal blood glucose levels, although not a level high enough to be classified to be a diabetic. Improving your glucose tolerance by eating more fish and seafood can help to prevent diabetes and reduce the release of the fat-storing hormone insulin.

* It's low in kilojoules

Seafood has a fairly low kilojoule and fat content compared to other meats. Getting the same amount of protein for fewer kilojoules is a real bonus for weight reduction. For example, a 150 gram flathead fillet has 1.5 grams of fat, 150 grams of skinless chicken breast has 6 grams of fat, and 150 grams of lean beef (rib eye) has 8.5 grams of fat. By having lean fish or seafood at least twice a week instead of other meats, you should be able to cut down on 8 to 15 grams of fat a week.

The omega-3 fats in fish and seafood are called 'essential' because they can only be manufactured by your body in small amounts. They need to be supplied from your diet. All seafood contains varying amounts of omega-3 fatty acids, including cheaper canned fish varieties such as sardines, salmon and tuna.

Science says: You can slim down with seafood

Nutrition research has shown that your health and weight can benefit from eating fish and other seafood regularly. There used to be a theory that humans stored the fat from fish in the same way that fish store fat, in the liver and muscle, rather than in their fat cells. However, research has shown that fish oils are just as likely to be stored in the fat cells, but are one of the first to be used as energy. This was further supported by two interesting animal studies. One was done on rabbits who were fed fish oils and it was found that the fish fat was five times more likely to be transported out of the fat cells and be used as energy compared to beef and dairy fats. Another study — on pigs — showed a greater level of fat loss after exercise on a high fish-fat diet compared to those on a saturated-fat diet.

But back to us human beings. A recent Australian study showed that a kilojoule-restricted diet combined with daily fish consumption is highly effective in reducing blood pressure, lowering triglyceride levels while increasing 'good' cholesterol levels and in improving glucose tolerance. Another study, published in the *International Journal of Obesity*, found that a low-kilojoule diet that includes fish results in slightly more weight loss compared to a similar low-kilojoule diet without fish.

Practical tips for eating more seafood

Fish and seafood are a diverse, healthy and incredibly delicious food group. It's also a food group that varies considerably in price, with some items out of reach for the budget conscious (such as lobster or abalone), while others are always good value. The tips are designed to help you include more low-cost seafood choices in your diet.

- Try to include at least two servings of fish or seafood every week.
  In general, the cheapest types of seafood include squid, octopus, mussels and canned fish. Keep a lookout for specials in the seafood section of your supermarket. You may also be able to find whole fish, some species of fish fillets and a marinara mix for around $10 to $12 a kilogram.
- Look for healthy cooking methods to minimise the kilojoule content of your seafood meals. The microwave or barbeque are a good choice, in addition to grilling, baking, steaming. Any weight-loss benefits from eating seafood are eliminated if it is battered, fried or covered in butter or a cream-based sauce.
- Wrap fish in a foil parcel along with green onions, soy sauce and a little honey and cook. Serve with steamed basmati rice and some Asian greens.

- Look for creative, healthy ways to add flavour to fish and seafood using herbs, spices and marinades, such as a combination of garlic, lemon juice, soy.
- While seafood extender is cheap (also known as seafood highlighter or crab sticks), it certainly is an acquired taste. If you don't mind the taste, use it in salads, curries, sandwiches, soups and side dishes.
- Squid and octopus are both ideal in green salads. Just marinate them in some white wine, garlic, paprika and a small amount of olive oil, and quickly sear them on the barbecue for a quick and tasty lunch.
- Use canned fish in sandwiches and wraps. Combine with lettuce, tomato, grated carrot, chopped chives and some low-fat mayonnaise on wholegrain bread.
- Use canned fish for a tuna casserole using corn, peas, tomato, onion and mushroom with light evaporated skim milk. You may need to thicken it with cornflour. Serve the casserole over basmati rice, and sprinkle with a little cracked black pepper, paprika and Parmesan cheese.
- To make Spaghetti Marinara (if you can find a reasonably priced marina mix), make a tomato pasta sauce with lots of added vegetables and bring to a simmer. Add the marinara mix and let it cook in the sauce for 3–5 minutes or until the seafood is cooked. Serve over cooked spaghetti accompanied by a crusty wholegrain roll.

CHANGES TO HELP YOU WITH YOUR WEIGHT LOSS	KILOJOULES SAVED	POTENTIAL WEIGHT LOSS OVER A YEAR
Eating low cost fish for seafood twice a week	290 a week	Close to 0.5 kilogram

How can it save you money?

Here's what I meant when I said 'conditions apply'. You need to choose the lower-cost seafood items to save money. For example, sandwich tuna can be less than $5 a kilo, while ham is between $12 and $15. Squid, octopus and mussels can be less than $10 a kilo, and so can some fish fillets (basa, hoki) and whole fish (snapper, pilchards, whitebait). This is a similar price to chicken, but cheaper than lamb or beef. Let's estimate that you could save $6 a week by having two meals a week with these types of seafood choice.

One final way to save money on fish is to catch it yourself. However, it is beyond the scope of this book, or the ability of this writer, to give you any advice on how to do that successfully. (I think my brother would disown me if I started giving fishing tips.)

MONEY SAVED EACH WEEK	POTENTIAL TOTAL YEARLY SAVING
Eating low-cost fish for seafood twice a week = $6 (approx.)	$312

Healthy fish and seafood recipes

WHOLE FISH AND VEGETABLE PARCELS

Serves 2 to 4, depending on the size of the fish

1 whole snapper
2 teaspoons crushed garlic
1 tablespoon mixed fresh herbs, such as basil, thyme, oregano or parsley, finely chopped
salt and cracked black pepper, to taste
1 tablespoon olive oil
1 tablespoon lemon juice
1 tablespoon balsamic vinegar
½ Spanish onion, sliced lengthways into thin wedges

1 red capsicum, sliced into wide strips
2 small zucchini, quartered lengthways
2 roma tomatoes, quartered lengthways
2 carrots, peeled and quartered lengthways

Preheat the oven to 180°C.

In a small bowl, mix together the garlic, herbs, salt and cracked black pepper, oil, lemon juice and balsamic vinegar.

To prepare the fish, make 0.5cm cuts, scoring the fish across the thicker part of the flesh.

Take a large piece of aluminium foil and fold it in half, making sure it is big enough to wrap the fish and vegetables, with a little extra to make a seal. Place half the vegetables in the centre of the foil and sprinkle with half the herb mixture.

Place the fish on top of the vegetables and then cover with the remaining vegetables.

Sprinkle the remaining herb mixture over the top. Wrap the fish, sealing the edges well by double-folding.

Place on a baking tray and bake in the oven for 30–40 minutes (depending on the size of the fish). To check to see if the fish is cooked, unwrap and press your finger into the flesh (be careful of the hot steam). If the fish springs back and flakes easily, it is ready. After removing the fish from the oven, let it stand for 10 minutes.

To serve, carefully open the foil parcel, remove the fish and serve on a platter for people to help themselves. Serve with a green salad or some steamed vegetables.

BARBECUED BABY OCTOPUS

Serves 4

1kg baby octopus, cleaned
250ml red wine
2 tablespoons balsamic vinegar
2 tablespoons soy sauce
2 teaspoons crushed garlic

2 tablespoons barbecue sauce
1 tablespoon olive oil
1 tablespoon fresh parsley,
    finely chopped

Combine the octopus, wine, vinegar and soy sauce in a saucepan and bring to the boil.

Reduce the heat to low. Cover and simmer for 20–40 minutes or until tender.

Remove the octopus from the marinade and place in a bowl with the garlic, barbecue sauce and olive oil, combining all ingredients thoroughly.

Cook the octopus on a hot barbecue for 4–6 minutes, turning occasionally, until lightly charred. Garnish with the parsley and serve with a green salad.

CREAMY TUNA CASSEROLE

Serves 4

spray of oil
1 small onion, finely diced
1 teaspoon crushed garlic
1 carrot, finely diced
½ medium red capsicum, finely diced
125g can corn kernels, drained
440g can tuna, drained and flaked
  with a fork
3 cups cooked macaroni

½ cup chicken stock
1 tablespoon fresh parsley,
  finely chopped
2 tablespoons cornflour
375ml can light evaporated milk
2 teaspoons grated Parmesan
  cheese
2 tablespoons dried breadcrumbs
1 teaspoon paprika

Preheat the oven to 180°C.

Spray a non-stick saucepan with cooking oil spray. Over medium heat, sauté the onion, garlic, carrot and red capsicum for 3 minutes. Add the corn, tuna, macaroni, chicken stock and parsley to the pan and stir well.

In a small bowl, combine the cornflour with a third of the evaporated milk and stir until smooth. Add the remaining milk to the tuna mixture while continuously stirring over a medium heat. Gradually add the cornflour mixture, stirring constantly until the sauce boils and thickens. Remove from the heat and pour into a large ovenproof dish. Sprinkle the top of the casserole with the Parmesan cheese, breadcrumbs and paprika.

Bake for 20–30 minutes or until the top of the casserole is golden brown. Serve with salad or steamed vegetables.

6. EAT MORE SOUP

How will it affect your weight?

A great way to reduce the kilojoule content of your diet and lose weight is to have lots of vegetable soups. Ideal for lunch, dinner or even as a snack, a thick, healthy soup can be very satisfying, and it is also low in kilojoules. Soup is a low-energy-density food because of its high vegetable and water content. For example, 100 grams of vegetable soup contains approximately 220 kilojoules, while 100 grams of potato chips have over 2100 kilojoules (nearly ten times the kilojoule content). In addition, soup is usually served hot, so people tend to eat it slowly and feel full afterwards. What's more, soup is packed full of vitamins and minerals, helping your metabolism, immune system and hormones function at their best.

However, only water- and vegetable-based soups will help you lose weight. Creamy soups with ingredients such as butter, sour cream, full-cream milk or cream are much higher in fat and kilojoules, and may actually trigger weight gain. Soup is also a great timesaver because you can make large batches, reheat it quickly or freeze the leftovers.

Science says: Soup speeds up weight loss

A study conducted at Penn State University found that people who had a first course of soup prior to lunch were able to reduce their overall kilojoule intake at lunch by 20 per cent. Importantly, the soup eaters felt just as satisfied after their lunch and did not compensate by eating more kilojoules at dinner. The soup seems to take the edge off hunger, which could work equally as well by having a soup entree before your evening meal. If the average person eats 6500 kilojoules a day, and lunch makes up 25 per cent of that, then you could potentially save 325 kilojoules a day. It's also good to see that there are more sensible weight-loss methods involving soup instead of crazy week-long soup binges and cabbage soup diets. If you know anyone who has been on a cabbage soup diet for more than 3 days, don't ever share an elevator with them.

Practical tips for eating more soup

Healthy soups are the perfect low-kilojoule, low-cost meal. They are a great way to prevent winter weight gain and a tasty way to include more vegetables in your diet. Following are some great ideas on how to get more soup into your diet. Why not experiment with your own recipes and vegetable combinations.

- Use canned soups as an easy soup base, and 'build'. Add extra vegetables, lean meats, legumes, wholegrains, herbs, spices and condiments.
- Making your own soups from scratch will give you complete control over what you are eating. Use whatever vegetables you have left in the fridge or include frozen vegetables.
- Add pulses, including beans, peas and lentils to your soups.
- Make a basic vegetable soup as a base, and then do something different to it each time you serve it up in a bowl. For example, you could throw in some fresh herbs, blend in some spices, add extra vegetables, throw in some lentils, add smoked chicken breast or chopped bacon, or serve with low-fat croutons.
- Have soup as an entree prior to lunch and/or prior to dinner to make it easier to reduce the portion size of your main meals. Alternatively, have soup as a main meal for lunch or dinner.
- Have soup on hand in the fridge or in individual portions in the freezer, to have as a snack between meals.
- If you have bread with your soup choose wholegrain bread, avoid using butter or margarine and keep your portions small.

CHANGES TO HELP YOU WITH YOUR WEIGHT LOSS	KILOJOULES SAVED	POTENTIAL WEIGHT LOSS OVER A YEAR
Having soup before lunch or dinner twice a week	325 a week	1 kilogram

How can it save you money?

Home-made soup is one of the true low-cost food staples. Soup itself would probably cost less per serve than most meals, so there are definite savings to be made. By having soup as an entree to either lunch or dinner, you will eat less of your main meal, and potentially save on your food bills. The calculations are based on the fact that the average person spends $25 a day on food, and lunch makes up 25 per cent of your daily food spend. For the annual savings figure, I have assumed that you could have soup before a main meal at least twice a week, which may occur a little more in the cooler months, and a little less in the warmer months.

MONEY SAVED EACH DAY	POTENTIAL TOTAL YEARLY SAVING
Having soup before lunch or dinner twice a week = $1.25 (approx.)	$130

Healthy soup recipes

CREAMY CHICKEN AND CORN SOUP

Serves 4

1 onion, finely chopped
1 tablespoon crushed garlic
2 tablespoons water
1 cup cooked, finely diced chicken
1 cup chicken stock
1 cup skim milk
440g can creamed corn

2 tablespoons finely chopped
    fresh herbs (such as basil,
    parsley, green onions, chives)
½ teaspoon paprika
1 egg, lightly beaten
salt and cracked black pepper,
    to taste

Place the onion, garlic and water in a saucepan and cook over a medium heat for 5 minutes or until the onion is soft and translucent.

Add the chicken, chicken stock, skim milk, creamed corn, herbs and paprika and bring to the boil. Reduce to a simmer and cook for 5–10 minutes, stirring occasionally.

Add the beaten egg just before serving, stirring it through with a fork until the soup thickens. Season to taste with salt and black pepper.

HERB AND LENTIL SOUP

Serves 4

spray of olive oil
1 onion, chopped
1 stalk celery, finely sliced
1 teaspoon minced garlic
3 carrots, peeled and finely diced
1 potato, scrubbed and finely diced
250g red lentils, washed and drained
400g can tomatoes, roughly chopped

1 cup chicken stock
1 cup water
⅓ cup finely chopped fresh herbs
(any or all of parsley, basil,
coriander)
salt and cracked black pepper,
to taste

Lightly spray a non-stick frying pan with olive oil spray and place over a medium heat. Add the onion, celery, garlic, carrots, potatoes and lentils and stir for 5 minutes or until the onions are soft and translucent.

Add the tomatoes, chicken stock and water and bring to the boil. Reduce the heat, cover and simmer for 20 minutes or until the lentils and vegetables are tender. Add more water if required.

Season with salt and cracked black pepper and stir in the fresh herbs. Serve immediately.

MINESTRONE SOUP

Serves 4 to 6

1 onion, finely chopped
2 teaspoon minced garlic
1 stick celery, finely sliced
½ cup chopped green beans (topped
    and tailed and cut into 2cm pieces)
2 medium carrots, peeled and
finely diced
3 cups beef stock (or 3 beef stock
    cubes dissolved in 3 cups of water)

410g can tomatoes, roughly
    chopped
410g can butter beans, rinsed
    and drained
1 cup peeled and diced sweet
    potato
salt and cracked black pepper,
    to taste

In a large stockpot, add the onion, garlic, celery, green beans, carrots and beef stock.

Add the tomatoes, beans and sweet potato, and bring to the boil.

Simmer for 1 hour until all the vegetables are tender.

Hint: Fresh tomatoes can also be used in this soup. If you don't have fresh tomatoes, a good-quality tomato pasta sauce can work just as well. Be creative and substitute your own choice of vegetables, such as zucchini, spinach, pumpkin, potato, cabbage, kidney beans, barley and a handful of cooked wholegrain pasta.

7. MAKE YOUR OWN WEIGHT-LOSS SHAKES

How will it affect your weight?

Health professionals such as doctors and dietitians sometimes use meal-replacement products to help people whose excess weight is placing their health at risk. Now pharmacies and even supermarkets are getting in on the act, offering a wide range of meal-replacement drinks. They are promoted as a quick and easy weight-loss solution, and a convenient way to eat well without cooking. Some are sold in ready-to-go containers, while others come as powders to be made up with water or skim milk. I must confess to being an early critic, thinking these were a short-term solution and therefore flawed. But there is now some scientific evidence (see 'Science says') to suggest that these products can help people get results over the long term. While I can't help but recommend real food over a meal-replacement drink, I do acknowledge that these programs appeal to people who want initial motivation from seeing fast results. For people juggling a hectic lifestyle, who have trouble exercising due to excess weight, or who really struggle to prepare healthy food, then meal-replacements drinks may be a suitable option.

A good meal-replacement drink can fill you up while tasting good enough to be something you don't mind having regularly. They are obviously a better choice than junk food or takeaways. And if you look at the ingredients list, there's no reason why you can't make your own meal-replacement drinks at a fraction of the cost. While the manufacturers would like you to think their shakes contain some secret fat-melting property, the reality is that nearly all the ingredients can be found at your local supermarket. In fact, one supermarket brand that costs $20 for a 425 gram tub is 55 per cent sugar and 41 per cent skim-milk powder. Making home-made weight-loss shakes is actually healthier and much cheaper.

Science says: Power shakes power up your weight loss

There is some research that proves using a meal-replacement shake in your diet can help with weight control. A study published in the *International Journal of Obesity* found that using meal-replacement drinks twice a day combined with one additional sensible meal over 12 weeks can help you lose about 7 per cent of your body weight. So if the average person weighs 80 kilograms, you could lose around 5.5 kilograms after 12 weeks. They also found that you can maintain the weight loss after 12 weeks by switching to one meal-replacement drink and two sensible meals a day. A review of six studies using meal-replacement products found that they can safely and effectively produce significant and sustainable weight loss, and improve your health. There's even research to show that you can benefit equally by making your own meal-replacement shakes. A study from the Commonwealth Scientific and Industrial Research Organisation (CSIRO) in Adelaide found that people did not lose any more weight when given whey protein power to use as a meal replacement than those given skim milk powder. In fact, people using the budget-friendly skim milk powder lost slightly more weight than those on the more expensive whey protein powder.

Practical tips for using meal-replacement drinks

While weight loss is a lot more complicated than simply drinking a smoothie, meal-replacement drinks can work as part of an overall healthy lifestyle plan. Following are some general guidelines on how to use meal replacements safely and effectively.

- One reason commercial meal-replacement drinks work is because they come in the right portion size. They train your eyes and stomach to become accustomed to smaller portions. When making your own drink, keep your portion sizes moderate. It's very easy to have too much. Measure out your serving and have a glass of water beforehand to reduce your stomach capacity.
- To save time, pre-mix the dry ingredients in a large batch. You can also put it into bags or containers in individual serving sizes so you can take it with you when you leave the house.
- Use a meal-replacement drink for the meals that cause you the most trouble (where you tend to eat the wrong foods or eat big portions).

For example, if you already eat a healthy breakfast, focus on replacing lunch or dinner.

- Over time, mix and match the meals you replace to maintain interest.
- Don't use a meal-replacement drink for more than two meals a day without medical supervision.
- Don't use meal replacements as a green light to eat junk at your other meals. Make your normal meals healthy to maximise your results and your nutrient intake. Most meal-replacement programs usually recommend a restricted-carbohydrate-and-fat diet in combination with the commercial drink.
- If you get hungry, eat fruit between meals for added nutrients and fibre.
- As you begin to lose weight, rely less on meal replacements. Drinking your food can only satisfy you for so long.
- After your weight has reduced, use meal-replacement drinks occasionally, such as when you are busy and tired and don't have time to cook.
- Speak to your doctor, pharmacist or nutritionist if you have any questions or concerns.

Practical tips for making your own meal-replacement drinks

Home-made weight-loss shakes are easy to prepare and quick to consume. To match the nutritional quality of the commercial varieties, your home-made drink should contain the following ingredients.

A protein source

This helps you to feel full while also stabilising your blood sugar levels. Protein also helps you to lose fat rather than muscle mass when you reduce your kilojoule intake. Examples include skim milk, skim-milk powder, low-fat yoghurt, soy milk, soy-milk powder and whey protein powder.

A quality grain source

This gives you sustained energy, nutrients and fibre. Examples include wheat-germ, psyllium husks, oats and oat bran. Allow these grains to soften by soaking them in water for a few minutes before blending. Cooked rice can also be used. Experiment with using more than one grain source. Thicker drinks that are full of dietary fibre make you feel fuller by slowing down the rate that your stomach empties.

A flavour source

This helps you to enjoy the taste of the shake. Options include honey, jam, fresh or frozen fruit (banana, strawberries, mango and berries all work well), cocoa, vanilla essence, ground cinnamon, ground nutmeg, malt powder, low-fat ice-cream and artificial sweetener. The lower the kilojoule content, the better.

- Experiment with different combinations of ingredients to find what you enjoy best.
- Try to use at least some fruit as a flavour ingredient to boost the nutrient and fibre content of your drink.
- If your fat and kilojoule intake is low, add LSA (lecithin, sunflower seeds and almonds) or nuts to your meal-replacement drink.

CHANGES TO HELP YOU WITH YOUR WEIGHT LOSS	KILOJOULES SAVED	POTENTIAL WEIGHT LOSS OVER A YEAR
Switching from a supermarket drink to home-made alternative for 12 weeks	0 kilojoules, but will fill you up so you eat less	Potential to lose slightly more weight with more fibre and less sugar
Switching from pharmacy drink to home-made alternative for 12 weeks	neutral	Potential to lose 3–5 kilograms from either drink over 12 weeks

How can it save you money?

To calculate the potential savings, I have assumed that you would be having two meal-replacement drinks a day for 12 weeks. My feeling is that after 12 weeks, you will probably want a break from the drinks for a while. Most programs recommend that you have two meal-replacement drinks a day for 12 weeks, and then switch to one a day after that. So the potential savings over 12 months are potentially a lot more than what I have calculated. While a home-made meal-replacement drink will have a similar kilojoule content, they are much cheaper. According to *Choice* magazine, the average price of consuming two pharmacy-style meal-replacement drinks a day is approximately $42 a week. That's about $3 per drink. The average price of the three home-made smoothie drinks (see page 172) is only $1.20 per serve. The cheaper supermarket drinks (which contain more sugar than anything else) are $1.50 per serve, whereas my Chocolate Powdered Shake recipe is approximately $0.80 a serve.

MONEY SAVED EACH WEEK	POTENTIAL TOTAL YEARLY SAVING
Switching from a supermarket drink to home-made alternative for 12 weeks = $9.80 (approx.)	$117.60
Switching from pharmacy drink to home-made alternative for 12 weeks = $25.20 (approx.)	$302.40

Meal-replacement drink recipes

WILD BERRY POWER DRINK

Serves 1

200ml skim milk
2 teaspoons psyllium husks
½ cup frozen berries

1 tablespoon skim milk powder
1 teaspoon berry jam (optional)
¼ cup crushed ice

Place the milk and psyllium husks in a blender. Allow the husks to soak for 3–4 minutes.

Add the berries, skim milk powder, jam, if desired, and ice, and process until smooth and creamy.

Drink immediately.

MALTED MANGO MEAL-REPLACEMENT DRINK

Serves 1

200ml skim milk
2 teaspoons quick cook oats
½ cup frozen mango pieces

1 tablespoon malt powder
1 teaspoon honey (optional)
¼ cup crushed ice

Place the milk and oats in a blender. Allow the oats to soak for 3–4 minutes.

Add the mango, malt powder, honey, if desired, and ice, and process until smooth and creamy.

Drink immediately.

BANANA AND CHOCOLATE MEAL-REPLACEMENT DRINK

Serves 1

200ml skim milk
2 teaspoons wheatgerm
½ cup frozen banana pieces
1 teaspoon cocoa

1 tablespoon low-fat yoghurt
1 teaspoon honey (optional)
¼ cup crushed ice

Place the milk and the wheatgerm in a blender. Allow the wheatgerm to soak for 3–4 minutes.

Add the banana, cocoa, yoghurt, honey, if desired, and ice, and process until smooth and creamy.

Drink immediately.

CHOCOLATE POWDERED SHAKE

Serves 1

This makes a portable powdered drink that allows you to use a shaker instead of a blender.

⅓ cup skim milk powder
2 teaspoons psyllium husks

1 tablespoon powdered
   chocolate drink

Mix the ingredients together. Store in a zip-lock plastic bag or other container.

When you are ready to make the shake, pour the dry ingredients into a shaker with 1 cup of water and a few ice cubes, if available. Allow the drink to stand for 3–4 minutes to soak the husks.

Shake until well mixed and drink immediately.

APPENDIX

Make your own calculations

Here's where you can put in all the tips that are relevant to your lifestyle and tailor the calculations to match your particular circumstance. This is your opportunity to customise *The Tight Arse Diet* to suit you, rather than battling to fit your lifestyle in with a diet.

LIFESTYLE CHANGE	PROJECTED KILOJOULES / WEIGHT CHANGE	PROJECTED SAVINGS
TOTAL		

WHAT MORE CAN I DO TO HELP YOU LOSE WEIGHT?

I am genuinely passionate about health, fitness and wellness, and I am driven to help people enjoy the benefits it has to offer. If I can be of any further help to you in any way, please don't hesitate to contact me. If you have any questions, queries or concerns about any of the weight-loss tips in this book, and how the information relates to your circumstances, why not send me an email? If you have a positive experience you'd like to share after following the strategies in this book, I'd love to hear from you too. I'll do my best to get back to you ASAP.

The better body update: A free weekly weight-loss newsletter

Do you like to stay up-to-date on the latest strategies, news, information, and research on weight loss? Why not subscribe to my free weekly email health tip — the Better Body Update. Every Monday morning, you'll receive an email covering the latest in fat loss, fitness, nutrition and motivation. I keep it very short, but also informative and practical. You can subscribe by going to my website, and you can also unsubscribe at any time.

Find out more

If you'd like to find out more about my qualifications, my online training, or read some of the weight-loss articles I have written over the years, please have a look at my website. You can also find out more about the other books I have written and download an extract. And don't be afraid to update me on your progress after following the weight-loss and money-saving tips in this book. You might even have some tips of your own you'd like to share.

Kind regards
Andrew Cate

email: info@andrewcate.com
website: www.andrewcate.com
postal address: Andrew Cate
13A Waterview Street,
Mona Vale NSW 2103, Australia

9780733327773